WORLD WAR ME

How to Win the War I Lost

DR. JAMAL H. BRYANT

1st Edition 2009 © Jamal H. Bryant and
Empowerment Publishing House

ISBN: 10: 0-9841768-0-2
ISBN 13: 978-0-9841768-0-9

For more information write to:

Jamal Bryant Ministries
1505 Eutaw Place
Baltimore, MD 21217

www.jamalbryant.org
www.myspace.com/jamalbryant
www.twitter.com/jamalbryant
www.worldwarme.com

Library of Congress Control Number: 2010921006

6 7 8 9 10 / 09

Printed in Canada

DEDICATION

Dedicated to all the brave men and women fighting,
and the families that are waiting for their return.

CONTENTS

FOREWORD

★

Unequivocally, without a doubt, the battle for our soul rages more intensely every day. Yet I have, for many years, been concerned that the church has a tragic propensity to shoot its wounded. I believe that these wounded soldiers have some insights to share that would help others of us not make similar mistakes. Their mistakes offer keen insight worthy of special mention—to the point that we should indeed open up the vaunted dialog desperately needed to shed light on the road to recovery. Thank God another wounded soldier, Jamal Bryant, shows his recompense. In this magnanimous book, he takes responsibility to show weakness during refinement. Furthermore, he wholeheartedly shows us how Satan seeks to bring us under his demise. He distinguishes between weakness and wickedness, which are often sutured together as one and the same in the minds of many people. Invariably, he showcases how life's seemingly awful moments can be turned the right way around. This book is astonishingly rewarding as it helps grant you the strength to not put up the white flag of surrender to the archenemy.

In trying to put it succinctly for all, Jamal, this human work of art, is a practitioner of spiritual insight. His book masterfully displays how we are often caught between opposing forces, whether they be life or death, good or evil. It is primed with spiritual knowledge imparted on a sensory level that makes you a powerful force. Jamal's formula for success is coming into honest recognition of the power within. A formula that is frankly invaluable. A formula filled with many "a-ha!" moments that will serve as a guiding light for years to come.

Most importantly, this book offers a healing salve for those who have injured the body with their conduct, and yet have fallen so in love with God that they would rather bear the reproach of His children than be permanently discharged from His service. The notion of "I will never leave a wounded comrade" could pass for just words until you stand amongst thousands of such generals who have placed the mission first. While many have withdrawn under intense, hostile enemy fire, Jamal has remained behind to counterattack and fight all the way to the grim to liberate one soldier, one family, and one church at a time. This book will keep you from backtracking due to fear. It will help you keep moving forward against the headwind of life's trials and travails—the ones that seek to put you into an emotional, mental and spiritual funk. To contend against that, READ this book in the spirit of meekness considering the power that reigns within because of HIM!

—Bishop T.D. Jakes, Sr.
Potter's House of Dallas

SECTION I

Chapter 1

WORLD WAR ME

★

You have only two things in life: your image and your integrity.

While I was a college student at Morehouse, one of my mentors expressed to me, "You have only two things in life: your image and your integrity." Regrettably, I only listened to half of what he said. I digested the part on image but discarded the part about integrity.

To the outside it would appear I had everything anyone would want. By thirty-five, I had obtained a Bentley, two houses on the water and consistent appearances on several television networks—BET, TV One, and TBN. I was looked upon as one of the upcoming leaders in the community and profiled in magazines and newspapers. I led a dynamic ministry of ten thousand members, all in under ten years. I also had a beautiful wife and gorgeous children, yet it was not enough.

Money was never an issue, but I did have issues. I flew around the world; preached; lectured; taught in coliseums, arenas and convention centers; and conducted conferences. I do not know the exact day, time, or moment I made image a priority and integrity an accessory, but it happened. Nor did I realize I was in a war every person is required to face—the fight between image and integrity. Every war has a price, and the cost of my battle was extremely expensive, almost to the point of having to file emotional, spiritual and psychological bankruptcy. I lost the trust of an exceptional wife, compromised the confidence of the Christian community, blemished the foundation of a strong family name, and jeopardized my relationship with the Lord.

By thirty-five, I had obtained a Bentley, two houses on the water and consistent appearances on several television networks

By writing this story, it is my intent and aim to assist every person whose eyes touch these pages to obtain an aerial view of the war you may not know you are in. When an alcoholic begins with Alcoholics Anonymous, the first step of the 12-step program is for the person to admit he has a problem. I admit the war never ends—every day is a struggle. Each day has within it a new battle. The good news is each day the war is winnable, but it is still war, and war many times has casualties. In this war, the casualties are divorce, debt, depression, distance, and disaster. In my war, I suffered all of these on the front line.

I never participated in ROTC (Reserve Officer Training Course), went to boot camp, or served in the Armed Forces. It was never my experience to have a sergeant awaken me early in the morning with a whistle. I was never assigned to a platoon nor did I spend one night on a military base. Due to this lack of training, I was neither able to recognize the war within me, nor did I know how to do battle against it. Immediate on-the-ground training was required if I was to survive. It is my hope that what took me years to learn, you will have a strong understanding of by the time you reach the end of this book.

★

Every war has a price, and the cost of my battle was extremely expensive, almost to the point of having to file emotional, spiritual and psychological bankruptcy.

★

World War I also known as the First World War, lasted from 1914 to 1918. It was fought between the Allied powers—Great Britain, France, and the United States of America—and the Central powers of Germany, Austria, and the Ottoman Empire. Regrettably it recorded nine million deaths. This war destroyed empires and redesigned maps.

As you go through the season of warfare, be prepared to see that at the end of the battle, empires will be destroyed, and the map of your life will have been redrawn. The direction you were taking before this battle will dramatically shift because God will alter your course as you align your attitude with His.

World War II endured from 1939 to 1945. This was the deadliest war in history. It embroiled Germany, Japan, and Italy against the United Kingdom, France, Poland, and eventually the United States. Sixty-two million people died during the course of World War II.

Experts on the science of warfare believe the next war launched will be World War III. They claim it will change the face of the Earth. Statisticians have in fact predicted a loss of five billion lives. The planet will not be recognizable if we go into World War III—water will not be drinkable, the air will not be breathable, and entire generations and families will be wiped out. If the people of God would have a mind of warfare, five billion souls can be saved.

Many years ago Albert Einstein was interviewed and asked, "What kind of weapons will be used in World War III?"

He said, "I don't know what kind of weapons will be used in World War III but if there is a World War IV, the weapons will be sticks and stones." The devil should know that this time we are not flirting with warfare, but we are going in without expecting another battle after this one.

While it is true a nuclear blast can wreak havoc on the world, the next war will not start in North Korea, Afghanistan, Iraq, or Washington. The next war is taking place right now, and it's entitled World War Me. There is an African expression, *Sankofa,* which means flying forward while looking back. To win this war, we can learn from the lessons of previous wars.

On August 17, 1955, President Dwight D. Eisenhower established the U.S. Code of Conduct, which is the legal guide for the behavior of military members who are captured by hostile forces. It is in six brief articles addressing those situations and decision areas that, to some degree, all military personnel could encounter. It includes basic information useful to U.S. Prisoners of War in their efforts to survive honorably while resisting their captor's efforts to exploit them to the advantage of the enemy's cause and their own disadvantage. It has been twice modified—once in 1977 by President Jimmy Carter and again in 1988 by President Ronald Reagan, who made the code gender neutral. The six articles state:

I am an American fighting in the forces that guard my country and our way of life, I am prepared to give my life in their defense.

I will never surrender of my own free will. If in command, I will never surrender the members of my command while they still have the means to resist.

If I am captured I will continue to resist by all means available. I will make every effort to escape and aid others to escape. I will accept neither parole nor special favors from the enemy.

If I become a prisoner of war, I will keep faith with my fellow prisoners. I will give no information or take part in any action which might be harmful to my comrades. If I am senior, I will take command. If not, I will obey the lawful orders of those appointed over me and will back them up in every way.

Should I become a prisoner of war, I am required to give name, rank, service number, and date of birth. I will evade answering further questions to the utmost of my ability. I will make no oral or written statements disloyal to my country and its allies.

I will never forget that I am an American fighting for freedom, responsible for my actions, and dedicated to the principles which made my country free. I will trust in my God and in the United States of America.

The Lord is giving us a code of conduct of how we are to conduct ourselves while in the middle of warfare. I will share with you six ways we are to conduct ourselves in the midst of this urban guerilla and inner-city warfare that is corrupting our children, stealing our men, and dividing our families.

The first code of conduct snatched out of the U.S. Army code of conduct is "I am a Christian fighting soldier. I serve in the forces that guard my community and destiny. I am prepared to give my life in their defense." If you are in God's army, declare this first code of conduct out loud. From 1988 to 1997 we had more black people dead over the cocaine drug cartel in our community. If they were able to die on a street corner, how come the body of Christ just wants to clap and shout and nobody wants to die? If you want to reign with Jesus then you have to be ready to suffer with him. Everybody wants to be blessed, but nobody wants to be persecuted; if you are willing to die for God, why are you not living for Him?

Article number two says, "I will never surrender out of my own free will. I will never surrender my neighbor if they still have a fight in them." This means whatever happens, quitting is not an option; I am not going to give up. It doesn't matter how the odds are stacked against me, I refuse to throw in the towel. I have been through too much to get to this point in my life and wave the white flag. Not only do I refuse to quit, but I am not going to sell out anybody connected to me. Anybody I know who has a dream, I am making a commitment to help them until their dream comes to pass. Hezekiah Walker sang a song, "I Need You to Survive." Surround yourself with people who are able to get you up when you feel like giving up. You have to make a conscious decision that you are going to stick to the plan whatever the cost and ask those who hold you accountable to help you do it. The problem is some people are too selfish; they want to be the only ones who make it.

Article number three says, "If I am captured, I will continue to fight, I will do everything I can to escape, and aid others to escape. I don't want anything from the enemy." If I am captured I will continue to fight. Even when I am going through a hard time, I am not going to give up on my dream. Even when bad news comes, I will stand there anyhow. When I start going through, I will fight harder. When the enemy gets me caught up in something, while I am in it, I will still be fighting. When people walk away from me, when the check bounces or when my family is against me, I am still going to fight. And not only am I fighting to get me out, but if I know anybody else who is going through the same struggle as me, I am committed to fight for them as well to get a breakthrough. While I am in bondage, I don't want anything from the enemy. I would rather struggle than get one dime from someone who is demonic. So, if for a while I have to suffer, at least my character is still intact. I want to be able to say when I get to the top that I didn't have to sleep with anybody, I was simply safe. My phone can get cut off, I can get evicted, my hair can go undone, I may need a manicure, but even if I've got nothing, I will still bless the Lord at all times.

You might be going through a financial crisis and you know somewhere you can get some money but the spirit in you refuses that way. Forget it; just wait on God.

Article number four says, "If I become a prisoner, I will keep the faith." Just in case the enemy gets me caught up in something, I will keep telling myself that somebody is on the way to get me out. Help is on the way. He may not come when I want Him to come, but He is an on-time God. I've got to keep the faith that God is going to get me out of this, even when the environment does not seem favorable. Hebrews 11:1 tells us, *"Faith is the substance of things hoped for, the evidence of things not seen."*

Article four continues, "If I am senior then I am going to take command that I am the ranking officer because I have been in it a long time." If you have only been through headaches then you are still underqualified. If I am not senior enough to be in control then I am going to fall in line behind somebody who outranks me.

Article number five says, "Even under distress, I will not speak negatively against my Savior, my shepherd, or my sanctuary; I do not want to encourage the enemy." Because you know who you are in the kingdom, never again after today allow anybody to speak against your church or your pastor in your presence. No matter how bad it gets, whatever happens in the church that you don't understand, do not put your mouth to it. If you don't like it, pray about it. It is a dangerous thing to talk about the anointed. The Bible tells us, *"Do not touch My anointed ones; do My prophets no harm."* (1 Chronicles 16:22, Psalm 105:15). The enemy hates the progress that has been made and the souls that have been saved. Look back over your life to where you were six years ago and see how much progress you have made. Things you used to do, you don't do anymore. Places you used to go, you don't go anymore. For me to speak negatively against my Savior, my shepherd, and my sanctuary encourages the enemy who wants to divide and conquer. We have to make a covenant that from this day we are sticking together. We are not in competition with anyone. The only thing we should divide is the kingdom of the enemy.

Article six says, "I won't forget what I am fighting for." When you are engaged in a battle, the enemy wants the battle to act as a distraction so that you take your eyes off what the true intent for your life is. Do not let what is happening to you stop your vision for what is ahead of you. Stay focused. *"Forgetting what is behind you, and straining toward the goal to win the prize for which God has called me heavenward in Christ Jesus."* (Philippians 3:13-14). Article six continues thus: "I will not forget what I am fighting for. I believe no matter what I will win." The fight is already fixed and the outcome predetermined, so do not wait till the battle is over. Rejoice in advance.

> ★
>
> *Do not let what is happening to you stop your vision for what is ahead of you. Stay focused.*
>
> ★

Chapter 2

FIGHTING FOR YOUR IDENTITY

———————————★———————————

Identity is who you are. Image is how you are viewed by others.

Identity theft has become the fastest growing criminal activity in the twenty-first century, replacing illegal drug sales. For the perpetrators, it offers the highest profit margin with the least risk, and for the victim, it causes incredible damage to their finances, credit, and peace of mind. In the United States alone, identity theft has reached fifty-three billion dollars a year. Consumers are directly shouldering about five billion dollars of that, but the rest, which is paid by businesses and retailers, is passed on indirectly to consumers who are paying more for goods and services.

Identity theft is a crime that involves someone else using your name, Social Security number, and other personal information. The theft can involve the use of your existing credit cards to make purchases or cash advances, opening new credit accounts in your name, or draining your financial accounts. It can even allow someone to use your name when they are arrested for criminal acts. Identity theft is a serious and growing phenomenon, and it is the number one concern of people contacting the Federal Trade Commission.

In recent months, there have been a rash of reports about big thefts, where criminals have stolen identities in mass quantities. Banks, credit card companies, and businesses that house servers storing passwords or other sensitive, private information have all reported break-ins that happened through the use of viruses and other online hacking methods, resulting in millions of pieces of information being stolen. There have also been instances of the information just getting lost, employees selling it, and other lax security measures resulting in thieves having access to your identity. The information can be used to obtain credit, merchandise, and services using the victims' name.

Identity theft can provide a thief with false credentials for immigration or other applications. One of the biggest problems with identity theft is that very often the crimes committed by the thief expert are often attributed to the victim.

There are two basic versions of financial identity theft:

1. **Victim Established Accounts Accessed.** The perpetrator pretends to be an existing account holder in order to obtain

funds from the legitimate bank account of the victim. This involves obtaining one or more identity tokens, then using it to access funds via an ATM, a telephone, or bank. If withdrawals, purchases, or checks are made against the victim's real accounts, that person will need to notify the bank that the debits are not legitimate and request reversal. At the extreme, the perpetrator may take over control of the account by rerouting statements to a new address. This is known as account takeover and opens the account to rabid abuse.

2. **Perpetrator Established Accounts.** The perpetrator establishes new accounts using someone else's identity or a made-up one. Typically the intent is to utilize someone else's good credit history to obtain funds or a checking account, which can be overdrafted. A classic example of credit-dependent financial crime occurs when a criminal obtains a loan from a financial institution by impersonating someone else and presents an accurate name, address, birth date, or other information that the lender requires as a means of establishing identity. Even if this information is checked against the data at a national consumer reporting agency, the lender will encounter no concerns, as all of the victim's information matches the records. The lender has no easy way to discover that the person is pretending to be the victim, especially if an original, government-issued ID can't be used for verification as is the case in online, mail, telephone, and fax-based transactions. This kind of crime is considered non-self-revealing, although authorities may be able to track down the criminal if the funds for the loan were

mailed to them. The criminal keeps the money from the loan, the financial institution is never repaid, and the victim is wrongly blamed for defaulting on a loan he never authorized.

According to Wikipedia, an account established by a perpetrator can be abused by passing bad checks, counterfeit money orders, or depositing empty envelopes into ATMs.

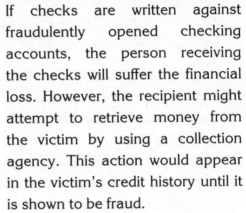

Is your identity your integrity or your image? What got me in the clutch of my crisis was having an identity crisis between the two.

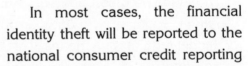

If checks are written against fraudulently opened checking accounts, the person receiving the checks will suffer the financial loss. However, the recipient might attempt to retrieve money from the victim by using a collection agency. This action would appear in the victim's credit history until it is shown to be fraud.

In most cases, the financial identity theft will be reported to the national consumer credit reporting agency or credit bureaus as a collection or bad loan under the victim's record. The victim may discover the incident when denied a loan, they see the accounts or they complain when they view their own credit history, or by being contacted by creditors or collection agencies. The victim's credit score, which affects one's ability to acquire new loans or credit lines, will be adversely affected until they are able to successfully dispute the fraudulent accounts and have them removed from their record.

The war is on. What's your true identity? Is your identity your integrity or your image? What got me in the clutch of my crisis was having an identity crisis between the two.

The underlying thing I had to learn is that my identity was not my image. Identity is who you are. Image is how you are viewed by others. Both influence the choices you make but identity offers much greater long-term rewards. Whenever possible, base your key life decisions on the person you are. Your identity should be your integrity. Let your identity be who you are when nobody is looking. Most people when they introduce themselves, they tell people what they do; and not who they are. The war you are in at this level is fighting to make your image your identity. A lot of people are facing foreclosure because they got into homes they knew they couldn't afford because they wanted image when their integrity should have convinced them to buy something smaller and build up their equity then buy something better when they could afford it.

You could lose a lot of money and your privacy could be violated, but identity theft as we use the term today, doesn't really result in the loss of your identity—of who you really are. That's not to say your identity can't be stolen or given away. Many of us give a great deal of thought to protecting our ID, our credit information, and our computer passwords, but we seem quite willing to give away our *true* identity. We willingly sacrifice our time, our energy, and our intellect to endeavors that are neither personally satisfying nor beneficial to humanity. We work at dead-end jobs; work on tasks that are demeaning and ill-paid, stripping us of our true identity, not allowing ourselves to live fully into the potential of God's original intent for our lives. We allow our quest for what the world tells us is the good life to destroy our dreams, hopes, and aspirations.

When it comes to recovering from identity theft, there is no one-stop solution. As it is, your identity—almost every aspect of it—must be handled by you. This is because in-person verification is often needed to reestablish who you are after your identity has been stolen. You can follow all the rules for reporting the crime and contacting creditors, but sometimes the problems just won't go away. The costs of identity theft can include spending hundreds of dollars and hours of your time trying to clean up your credit history. Victims of identity theft may get little help from authorities who don't always have the resources to investigate these cases. With millions of cases reported each year, police and other agencies rarely get involved unless your case amounts to an exceptionally large theft.

Going through identity theft recovery is emotionally draining. Many victims suffer symptoms similar to those who survive an assault or other serious crimes. You may feel both helplessness and rage at your situation, as well as loss of financial security.

Most people will hardly stop wondering where all the money they had went, how they spent the money, and whether all the items they bought were necessary. These are good questions to ask yourself when you are already in bad debt. There are various reasons that lead many people into debt. More than fifty percent of the people in these situations overspend on their credit cards, and after some time, they become bankrupt. Other people don't actually know how to budget their finances, so they overspend what they normally earn. Most people shop their way into debt because of the images they see on commercials and in magazines. The truth of the matter is, you cannot run away from your problems. People must be responsible for their own financial trouble so that they are able to solve them.

Lately, the number of people inclined to have cosmetic surgery is increasing. Even when everyone is aware of the risks and dangers of plastic surgery, more and more people are raring to go for such treatment. Nearly eleven million, seven hundred thousand cosmetic surgical and nonsurgical procedures were performed in the United States in 2007, according to statistics released by the American Society for Aesthetic Plastic Surgery. They further state that the overall number of cosmetic procedures has increased four hundred fifty-seven percent since the collection of the statistics first began in 1997.

People have risked and lost their lives and limbs and suffered devastating disfigurement and scarring as a result of plastic surgery gone wrong. The worst outcomes are rare, but risk is nonetheless a reality, and it's all done for the purpose of image. For many patients, successful plastic surgery can lead to an increase in self-esteem and confidence, which can have a snowball effect on many areas of one's life. Often, the correction of a problem perceived by the patient can mean an increase in self-esteem and may make them more outgoing. Ironically, to most, it creates a completely changed person, so much so that they live with their friends without being identified.

You go through identity battles because the enemy wants to embroil you in illegal cloning. He wants you to fit in with the masses. But when God puts purpose in your life, He is letting you know you are fearfully and wonderfully made, cut out for that specific purpose. So, you have to fight for your own uniqueness. Do not let anybody break you or make you compromise the creativity God put in you. Anyone who does not like your personality, size, or appearance should not be permitted to influence you into being who you are not.

As pastor and preacher, I have done altar calls for people who needed emergency assistance with housing, cars, and utilities. Invariably, every time I do it, there is somebody who won't come to the altar for prayer but will try to come to me privately because they don't want to ask for help publicly. They think it will be a mark on their image. This is what happens with the identity and image struggle. In private, all of their self-assured control leaves and they are reduced to their helpless reality. If we don't learn how to live from the place of our true identity, we will pay the price in needs and lack until we do learn how to live.

It was a matter of identity theft that Jacob went up and dressed like Esau to cheat his brother out of his rights and privileges as Isaac's firstborn son. Ancient customs entitled the firstborn male to a special birthright and blessing from the family patriarch, which amounted to receiving the largest inheritance and assuming headship of the family after the father's death.

When Esau realized what Jacob had done and what all that he had lost, he was devastated. Identity theft or loss is a very personal and traumatic experience. When something that defines you–an account number, job position, a family role, social status, a beloved possession, etc.—is stripped from you, suddenly it can leave a terrible, terrible scar.

That wound cut deep for Esau. There was no canceling the initial birthright and issuing a new one. The deal was done. His brother permanently supplanted him as heir apparent to his father's wealth and authority.

Instead, I had stolen my own identity. So now I had to go to war with myself to reclaim my identity.

When I came to terms with myself, I realized it wasn't a hacker online who had stolen my identity nor a criminal who had stolen my wallet, intercepted my mail, or gone through my garbage. Instead, I had stolen my own identity. So now I had to go to war with myself to reclaim my identity.

Chapter 3

THE FIGHT IS ON!

———————★———————

Make plans by seeking advice; if you wage war, obtain guidance.

—Proverbs 20:18

There is an old saying that your attitude predicts your altitude. Basically, the way you think will project where you will end up. Though this may sound good, sometimes this will not work, especially for a person who is simply gifted but not grounded. Many times, doors of opportunity swing open before us, and as chance would have it, we rise to the occasion and walk through those doors. Owing to deficiency in our attitudes, however, we often find ourselves ejected through the very doors that could have recreated our destiny.

Growing up, particularly while in the forth grade, I always vied for a position of excellence. However, after getting into a gifted and talented program, it was my attitude that always retarded my progress. I had a behavioral problem; I was either the class clown, talking excessively, not doing my homework, or sheer irresponsibility in handling the assignments given to me. Proverbs 18:16 says your gift will make room for you, and indeed it will, but depending on your attitude, the room can become increasingly smaller with the walls coming in. This is precisely what befell me in the fall of 1985.

> *I had a behavioral problem; I was either the class clown, talking excessively, not doing my homework, or sheer irresponsibility in handling the assignments given to me.*

I entered the Baltimore City College Preparatory High School, one of the oldest high schools in the United States of America. My father and my uncle were inducted into the hall of fame for that high school. I was in the eleventh grade and when I entered the school, and I was marked among the gifted and talented— what W. E. B. Du Bois calls the talented ten. I was part of the class that was marked for excellence and was sure to go on to college by default—or so I thought. Well, somehow I underestimated the power of the high standards of excellence and the resulting power of high expectations. My teachers, knowing my gift and seeing what my previous test scores, knew I could perform and do well. But because I thought my gift would take me somewhere that discipline was not required, I never quite hit the mark.

As a consequence, the report card that came in the mail at the end of my junior year was shocking. Baltimore City High School had decided to retain me, not even in the core classes. Because it was two elective classes, there was no summer school option. Therefore, I was forced to repeat the eleventh grade, thanks to my poor attitude!

Thankfully, opportunity smiled on me again. By the grace of God, my father was elected bishop of the African Methodist Episcopal (AME) church. In the AME tradition, once one is first elected as bishop, their first assignment is always overseas. His first assignment then, was to be the jurisdiction director of the Fourteenth Episcopal District, which comprises Liberia, Nigeria, Sierra Leone, and Côte d'Ivoire. Upon that appointment, he made an announcement that as a family we were to move to Africa. My parents did not have a clue as to why I was so excited, and their attempts to figure it out would prove to be futile. I was excited, not because of foreign missions, not even because of outreach in a broad sense, but rather because I was able, in my mind, to escape the shame and humiliation of repeating a grade right before my peers, who by the way, were progressing.

In October 1988, we moved to Monrovia, the capital city of the western African nation of Liberia, which was never colonized by any European nation. It was founded by ex-slaves. When we moved there, I had an eye-opening experience that was to remarkably impact the rest of my life. In Liberia there was no public school system, so it was not altogether unusual to find twenty-four-year-olds and nineteen-year-olds in the sixth grade. Not because they were held back or retained. It was just the right time when they had enough crude oil to go to school.

So when I went to the American Co-operative School, which was hosted by the embassy, I made friends all over Liberia, and they were bewildered by how I had been retained for an education that was free, yet they were working their whole life to pay for education. This gave way to understanding that the Afro Negro Fund is absolutely correct in saying that a mind is a terrible thing to waste. it should not be a slogan per se, but it must be a lifestyle. From that moment until this hour my perspective on matters of attitude, discipline and submission have shifted because I understood at last, that to whom much is given, much shall be required.

And so there I was–my academic prospects hanging in the balance—in the thick of a battle that I was, like many, unconscious of, like many others. It was a battle not against armed foes from without, but one that raged from within between my giftedness on one hand and a slothful attitude on the other. People and life as a whole held me accountable for my gift, yet my attitude evidently turned out to be my own handicap. There can never be room for a person's gift to go forward until their handicapped attitude is straightened out.

After a year in Liberia, still in the eleventh grade, an older man who was a graduate of Morehouse College in Atlanta told me he had found out about an early college program at Morehouse and recommended that I spend the summer of 1989 at the school. It was a summer that would groom students preparing to enter their senior year. I went and performed very well, casting into the highest five percentile of everybody in the program. I shared with the advisor that I had been retained and had to wait another year to attend. That advisor, under the very hand of God – I believe–advised me not to wait another year. I was encouraged, rather, to go get a General Equivalency Diploma (GED). Following the advice, I went to the community college, enrolled in the class and took my GED without ever attending a GED prep class. When the grades came back two weeks later, I had scored in the top five percentile in the nation of everybody who took the GED. It proved to me again that I had the gift, but without discipline, the gift could amount to absolutely nothing. So in a brutal act of faith I applied to Morehouse five weeks before the semester was supposed to begin. Everybody tried to contaminate my hope and said that it could not happen. Morehouse was a school that had never admitted students who had a GED, so I figured that I may not make it in.

People and life as a whole held me accountable for my gift, yet my attitude evidently turned out to be my own handicap.

The first, second, and third weeks went by without any word. My father, at the end of the third week, told me to pack my bags. I was to head back with my family to Liberia and return to school there. With tears in my eyes

I implored him not to make me go back, that I knew with everything in me I was supposed to attend Morehouse. He said maybe I was supposed to be in Morehouse, but it would be in a year because I didn't do well enough in high school, and my attitude was deplorable. With focus and a firm determination, I persevered and entered Morehouse College that year.

★

All great battles have always had a name based on location—the Battle of Wounded Knee, the Alamo—and there is a war ensuing that will be entitled in time and eternity as World War Me.

★

You are about to enter full-scale warfare, and this time, it is for your life! All great battles have always had a name based on location—the Battle of Wounded Knee, the Alamo—and there is a war ensuing that will be entitled in time and eternity as World War Me.

It is very important for you to realize that the war you are about to enter has nothing to do with you, but because you have purposed to be supernaturally successful, the battle lines have been drawn. If you are complacent and comfortable with living a mediocre life, the enemy will not bother with you, but because you have looked beyond the grass and seen the hills, the enemy has engaged you into a war you have never fought before. The second war was lost because a lot of people looked beyond the fringes and fought for power.

Different from what we see happening now, the battle you are entering into has nothing to do with money and it has nothing to do with human capital. The devil is not after your finances because you don't have enough, but he values your human resource. Do you realize how much of a threat you are to the kingdom of darkness? The enemy can't afford for you to ever get into a place of prosperity. You are in fact a threat to the enemy on a job you don't like. Can you imagine how much more a threat you would be to the kingdom of darkness if you were to go into a career that you enjoyed? You are a threat to the enemy when you don't know your purpose. Can you imagine how intense the attack will be when you walk into your purpose? You are a threat when you are not happy with life now. Can you imagine how intense the attack will be when you finally find the happiness that the world cannot give and neither can they take it away? You are a threat to the enemy, yet you don't even read your Bible every day. Can you imagine how much more the enemy will go after you when you become diligent and disciplined in the faithful reading of the Word of God? You are a threat to the enemy and you don't tithe every Sunday. Can you imagine how much more the enemy will pursue you when you understand that the Lord wants your reasonable portion?

The mistake America made in the Vietnam exchange was that America never declared war. As a result they were never able to declare victory. I proclaim in the face of the enemy, "I declare war!" We plan to win with our entire family. When you understand the destiny and the call that is on your life, you can't afford to be an onlooker while war is being waged.

When you come to realize that the enemy is trying to destroy our men, women, children, and generation, then you know it's time to roll up our sleeves and declare war.

Different from World War I, this war is not focused on topography or geography. This war has only one target: to kill your dream, your ambition, your drive, and your passion. However, the enemy messed up by bringing the wrong weapons. He thought our weapons were simply carnal, but the weapons of our warfare are *not* carnal. They are mighty through God to the pulling down of strongholds and casting down of every imagination that exalts itself above the knowledge of God (2 Corinthians 10:3-5). When we are going through battle, we don't have to pull out an AK-47. On the contrary, we have to know how to talk to God in the midst of our battles.

When you go into warfare, prepare to fight. Minister Jonathan Nelson, a Stellar Award winner, wrote a song that says, "My praise is my weapon." Many of us only use praise when we have the victory, but we fail to understand that we have to praise God even when we are under attack. While you go through the fight of your life, praise God like it is the only weapon left.

In no uncertain terms, this war is completely about your supernatural success. The enemy wants to bar you from being successful. If your dreams weren't so big and if your focus wasn't so clear, you wouldn't be going through what you are facing. I wouldn't want to be anyone else in the world but me. That's why if I must go down, it will not be without a spirited fight. Let me go down fighting—fighting for my dream to become reality.

A Chinese writer once said, "When you are engaged in warfare, you have to make the enemy psychologically frustrated." You have to make the enemy believe you are winning even when it seems like you are losing. The enemy might have beaten you on the job or in marriage, but be determined to praise your way out. You have to confuse the enemy. When the enemy throws his hardest blow at you, when he thinks you should be complaining and cursing God, but he finds you praising instead, it makes him run out of ammunition.

Different from World War I, this war is not focused on topography or geography. This war has only one target: to kill your dream, your ambition, your drive, and your passion.

According to Robert Greene, a Jewish American author known for his books on strategy, power, sex, and seduction, "You must take control over people's perceptions of you by playing with appearances, mystifying, and misleading them. It is best to mix audacity with unpredictability and unorthodoxy and act boldly in moments of weakness or danger. That will distract people from any holes in your armor, and they'll be afraid there may be more to you than meets the eye. Then, if you make your behavior hard to read, you will only seem more powerful since action that eludes interpretation attracts attention, worry, and a bit of awe. In this way you will throw people off.

Aggressors will back off..." In other words, your appearance and your enemy's perception of you as someone not to mess with will soon become a reality and get the enemies onto their heels. Now, this kind of thinking

---

★

Don't react on the basis of where you are, but on where you are going. That is how we succeed in confusing the enemy

★

---

is certainly unseemly for those who still think their enemy is the girl next door, the harsh boss at their workplace or somebody who said this or did that when they were young. To us who know that we wrestle not against flesh and blood, this is one of the best ways to disable our enemies; these are principalities and powers of darkness under the auspices of Satan himself. In life we all encounter people who do hurtful things to us. But if we quickly recognize these are in fact not our real enemies, it would alert us of the need to get better equipped for the *real* war.

In the side mirror of automobiles, there is a sticker that says, "Objects may be closer than they appear." Your issue is closer than what it appears to be. Most of us try to act like our vulnerability or weakness is a great ways off. It is actually much closer than we realize. It is reflected in the way we dress each morning, the conversations in which we participate, the emails and text messages we read and forward on to others. The struggle of vulnerability follows us through our daily lives and makes up a portion of our personality and standards.

Don't react on the basis of where you are, but on where you are going. That is how we succeed in confusing the enemy who, as we know from scripture is the author of confusion, thus beating him by his own invention. When you are penniless, praise God like you are debt free; if you are jobless, go buy a briefcase; if you don't have a car yet, go buy yourself a gas card; act like you already have what you need and that which you desire.

It is very important to get our minds renewed and adapted to the fact that we are fighting a defeated enemy. The reason we have already won is because blood has already been shed for that victory.

When you are faced with disorienting situations, do not imagine that something totally unusual has befallen you. As a matter of fact, you will often come across people who tell you that whatever you are trying to achieve can't be done. We all do encounter such negative people at one time or another. But remember your attitude is key, and in order to win the war you have to use your mind, *not* your emotions.

It is very important to get our minds renewed and adapted to the fact that we are fighting a defeated enemy. The reason we have already won is because blood has already been shed for that victory. I thank God that it was not my blood, but thousands of years ago, on a hill called Calvary. They hung the Son of the Most High God, Jesus Christ, high and stretched Him wide. This blood was poured out to cover the generations of those who lived and those who were not yet born. It's been thousands of years since and yet even to this day, no matter what kind of battle we find ourselves in, we can always count on that same blood to see us through. Back in the day, whenever the people of old were in trouble, they would say, "The blood of Jesus," or "Devil, the blood of Jesus is against you." We can borrow from them. We are sure to win because the blood of Jesus is fighting for us against our enemy. Amazingly, it does even more. The blood of Jesus does not only cover us, but also our families and those that relate to us in various ways. All we have to do is ask.

Once upon a time, I was lost. But now I am found. Jesus died on the cross and I know it was the blood that saved me. If you are not saved, you have a reason to be nervous, very nervous. Because you know Jesus died for you, you too can always turn to Him, and as a result, you will be able to get up every morning and concur with the timeless song that says, "Because he lives I can face tomorrow."

The battle was already won when the enemy tried to make Jesus a casualty of war. What the devil did not plan for was that He would get back up. The enemy may have dealt some hard blows on you, which may have put you down, but remember you have the power to rise again through Him who lives in you. After all, greater is He that is in you than the devil who is in the world.

If you desire anything, you have to be prepared to fight for it. If you do not need anything, then you will not get anything, and as such, you won't have to fight. But if you desire something, then war is inevitable. As a matter of fact, the war is already in progress, but now that you are still alive and hidden in the blood, know that everything the devil is trying to do to destroy you is bound to fail. As a believer, you have a promise: no weapon formed against you shall be able to prosper (Isaiah 54:17).

Writer, Robert Greene, provides a working definition that can aid us in distinguishing between a strategist and a tactician. Strategists look at the entire plan of the military operation, while tacticians look at the battle all by itself. You are strategically positioned by God, who has the big picture of the entire operation. He has positioned you in such a way that if you would submit to His strategic plan for your life, He will strengthen you to handle whatever you are going through so that it will not break you. People who observe you casually may see what you are going through and think that that's all you have. But if you have your destiny in clear perspective, then you know what you are experiencing is a small battle compared to the larger war, which by the way, you are certain to win. What you are going through right now is not going to stop anything that the Lord has lined up for you. If God didn't have any purpose for you, you would be dead by now; but because He is not through with you yet, you are still alive. You will behold the goodness of the Lord in the land of the living.

Keep the attitude of an overcomer. Solomon told his son he was connected to him; he had his blood, his promise, and his wealth, but that did not mean the son would not have to engage in any of his father's battles. Because you are saved does not mean you will not face any fights. You will. The difference is your victory is sure. The enemy is only after you because you have a blood relationship with Jesus. Solomon advised his son to get some right-minded soldiers—people who do not easily get intimidated. Likewise, get yourself connected with people who will stay with you when times are tough. You need more warriors around you than spectators. This war you are embroiled in is too big for you to handle by yourself. If you have the right advisors around you—the kind who will consistently urge you to move your attitude in the direction of your destiny, then you can win the war.

Chapter 4

I'VE BEEN DRAFTED

———————★———————

It is the responsibility of every person going through warfare to know that you cannot run from the place of your assignment.

Typically a draft occurs when a conflict requires more troops than the military has at the time. In order for a draft to be placed into operation, Congress has to pass legislation then the President has to sign the law into effect. More often than not, it is random, that is selective service. You are given a number, and when your number has been called, you must report to your local military station. You then go through a battery of exams that will test your physical, moral, and mental aptitude.

In the midst of my crisis, I began to sing one of the greatest hymns ever written, entitled "Why Me?" I could not believe I was losing my family, facing public shame, and being discussed on thousands of blog sites. My speaking engagements were cancelled, I had to apologize to my own conference, and I deeply wounded my parents.

Have you noticed we normally ask "Why me?" only when something bad happens? Why do we not ask the same question when something good happens? I didn't ask, "Why me?" when, within four years, six thousand people joined the church I pastored. Nor did I ask, "Why me?" when I was invited to preach at one of the largest Christian conferences, or when an elementary school in Africa was named for me, not even when the school I dropped out of invited me to be the commencement speaker.

Have you noticed we normally ask "Why me?" only when something bad happens? Why do we not ask the same question when something good happens?

One danger of being gifted and having the call of God on your life is to be convinced that you deserve the best, that anything less is not good enough. When Lazarus was pronounced dead, Jesus told his friends and family it was not an ultimate death, but instead it was for His glory. At the time, I could not see it, but now I realize God would use my trial as a testimony for those who are engaged in *World War Me*.

It is the responsibility of every person going through warfare to know that you can't run from the place of your assignment. You can't be like Jonah who didn't want to go to Nineveh and wound up in the belly of a whale. Understand that sometimes the problem is not in the man, but rather in the land, and when you change your environment, your inner man changes.

On December 20, 2001, Nick Smith, a Republican Congressman from Michigan, introduced the Universal Military Training Act of 2001. This called for the induction of young men into the Armed Forces who were registered under the Military Selective Service Act. Also, this authorized young female volunteers to receive basic military training and education for up to one year. He went before the congressional floor and said, "America faces a unique moment in history, our nation is at war, our homeland was attacked, and our personal security is more at risk than it's been since World War II. A draft is necessary..."

I earnestly declare that a draft has to be evoked. There is an under-current of attacks bombarding the Kingdom of God. When you look at the rise in popularity of the *Da Vinci Code,* you can see that the Kingdom is under attack. When CNN reports, as its banner story, that Jesus *didn't* walk on water, but walked on ice, the church is under attack. I really don't have to go through the headlines. A look at your own life should provide all the evidence you need. Look at what you have had to endure and go through since you were saved. Understanding that your body is a living temple, that you must live a holy and acceptable life, and you find yourself dealing with sickness, fatigue, and stress; then you know you too are under attack.

The Lord is searching for people to draft. Not just anyone will do. He is selective, looking for those who will serve capably in His army. In case you didn't know, the Lord has been recently walking you through various trials to see whether you would stand the test of time. He had to allow you to endure some physical tests, sicknesses, soul drain, and pain. An ordinary person would have found a way to end their life, but you are still here and in your right mind. Perhaps you've had an attitude, and you may not even know why you're angry and crying. Maybe you don't even know from where the tears were coming. God has taken you through moral tests, where He places you in various situations to show how you've grown; whether you would fall for the same things that you fell for prior to the testing of your faith.

It's not necessary to have all the answers to ensure you pass the test. You pass the test if you did better this semester than you did the last term. Be sure to take pleasure in knowing how much you have developed and grown.

In Judges 6, God dealt with a people claiming to have faith but they were fickle. They did what was seemingly right in their own eyes; but always ended up in bondage. After finding themselves enslaved, they would go through a season of repentance and prayer; then the Lord would give them relief and a break-through. After this they would go into revival and praise God for their escape from captivity.

But soon, the revival would end. They would start the cycle over again, walk in disobedience, fall into bondage, then cry out for help. Is this not like many of us? The Lord will bring us out of a situation. We will shout and praise for a while, but then we return very thing the Lord delivered us from. He wants to draft those who will fight to turn this around and elevate their standard of consciousness; people who will lead and stand in the gap for others.

God drafted a young man named Gideon. He told Gideon to lead the army even though he had no military experience, and didn't know how to handle military weaponry.

Whenever God calls you, He calls you to do something you have not been doing before.

By experience and certification Gideon was not a soldier but a farmer. Whenever God calls you, He calls you to do something you have not been doing before. He calls you to do something you have no experience, education, or training for but just wants to see if you will trust Him. Many have run from the call saying they can't do it. God will call you into service, and the only way you will be successful is if you take Him with you.

Gideon said, "How can I save Israel? My clan is the weakest in Manasseh, and I am the least in my family." (Judges 6:15) In other words, "Lord, get somebody else. I come from a family that is broken; I come from a family

41

where nobody has done anything great; I come from a family where nobody has ever thought outside the box."

But God said to Gideon, "That's why I chose you. I chose you because I want people to understand that when you get to this level of success, it has nothing to do with who your family is, or who your contacts are or what your last name is. I am looking for people whose families are junked up so that when I bring them out, they'll going to bring their whole family out with them."

★

Stop praying all the time and start fighting some of the time. Prayer is good but sometimes you've got to do more than pray.

★

It's a difficult thing to have a call on your life with a family that is dysfunctional. It's fanatical to have high expectations when you've come from a family with low aim. But God will use you to shift the family curse. The strongholds that have been holding your family back for years, will fall away when He brings you through. Nobody in your family will have to settle for second best ever again. God will use you to raise the level of excellence. He told Gideon (Judges 7, paraphrased), "I am making you the general of the army; with no experience, training, or expertise." Then Gideon said, "I can do it because I have thirty-two thousand soldiers." Then the Lord said, "You think all the people around you are with you? Don't think that because people are around you that they are down for you! You

really don't know who is with you until it is time to fight."
Gideon knew that the enemy was outnumbered his army
four times over. But God said, "What good would the army
be if in the middle of the battle they don't feel fighting.
Send them home and when they leave, don't cry because
they will do more damage by staying. Let them leave now
before the battle gets fierce. Stand right there; watch
them leave and wave!"

   The army's size dropped from thirty-two thousand to
twenty-two thousand. The ratio now had become to eight to
one. Then God told Gideon to take them down to the water,
and those who got on their knees and started drinking are
not the ones, send them home. For some people, all they
can do when in battle is drop to their knees. God says, "You
have prayed enough; now that you have the answer, get up
and handle your situation." Stop praying all the time and
start fighting some of the time. Prayer is good but sometimes
you've got to do more than pray. Faith without works is dead.
You have prayed, read the Word, and now it's time to fight.
Those who simply stay on their knees are presumably too
spiritual for this. You need some people around you who are
practical. If they can't handle it, leave them at church! Much
like those who have smoked for twenty years and quit and
then someone comes smoking; they begin to cough and act
as though they've not been around it before. Maybe you have
only been saved three weeks, but you're already pointing
fingers at people and telling them how they're going to hell.
I'd like to know how it is you are able to speak in tongues but
you can't speak to me.

Gideon sent all of them home. All he had left was three hundred soldiers–reduced from thirty-two thousand– comparatively speaking is less than one percent of the army's original size. Take the three hundred and prepare to go into battle. All we need are three hundred draftees, certified enough, through enough tests who will declare, "For God I will live and for God I will die." After God selected three hundred soldiers, He chose three weapons with which they were to fight: a jar, a torch, and a trumpet. Gideon asked God how he was going to fight with an empty jar, a torch, and a trumpet. God instructed him to let each of the three hundred men take their jar and hit it against the jar of the person beside him. It is important for you to understand that we are treasures in earthen vessels—God is the potter and we are the clay. Their first weapon was a jar made out of clay, which they had to break. You will never be able to fight wholly for God until you are broken. When the two jars collide – remember they are empty – there was a lot of noise when they shattered. When broken by people close to you and you are wounded, you will shout.

Then God told them to take the torch and place it in the broken vessel. Let your light so shine among men, God says, "Let your light shine before men, that they may see your good deeds and praise your Father in heaven." (Matthew 5:16). The light signifies knowledge, wisdom, and understanding. God wants to let us know that He does not put the light in us until we are broken. This means some of the things that wounded you were school for you. God was teaching and training you in the middle of your pain so you could learn what you could live with and what you could do without. "I am going to put the light in you so that when your enemies are far off, they will not be able to see you but they *will* see the light *in* you," God says. There are people looking at you and wondering how you've been able to keep it together even when life has been falling apart.

Then he gave them a trumpet saying that there were more in the enemy's camp than there were of them; but if the three hundred blew their trumpet at the same time, they would sound like thirty-two thousand. They had to blow the trumpet three times. The first time was a signal to their enemies; they were on the way. The second time an announcement: "Negotiations over, the war begins NOW!" The third time daclared that reinforcements were behind them—they were not alone.

The Bible says in Judges 7 that when the sound was made, the enemy fled. Three hundred of them, because of their shout and praise, handled the fight for thirty-two thousand, so that when the enemy ran, they were making a way for the thirty-one thousand, seven hundred who were left at home. If you shout, God is not just going to bless you, but He will bless even those you left at home—those who wouldn't even praise Him. Anybody who is tired does not have to participate. Whether you like it or not, you've been pulled into this.

Chapter 5

I'M BORN FOR THIS

A friend loves at all times, and a brother is born for adversity.

—Proverbs 17:17

It is interesting that animals were created with instinctive defensive mechanisms—things that would help them to survive the environment into which they were born. They were created with all the tools necessary for them to brave natural elements. Take the goldfish, for example, nobody had to teach them how to swim. They were born into an environment where they could not only survive naturally, but they'll thrive. A bear doesn't have to go through wilderness training; he instinctively knows how to handle his natural habitat.

Humans, however, were not born with such an advantage. No matter what the environment, the human is dependent on someone providing for and teaching them how survive, perhaps even to thrive. Somebody must show them exactly how to brave the elements and how to endure through tough circumstances. One differing aspect between humans and animals is that a human's best chance for survival is to be engaged in groups of other people, known as communities. Society ought to cultivate an environment where you are to learn, worship, and govern yourself with law, justice, and equality. It is in this populace that you live, you are shown how to find shelter and how to aim for more in your life. The social order has, however, become contaminated because we have lost the sense of group dynamics. There is, in fact, a saying that it takes an entire village to raise a child; however it becomes increasingly difficult to raise that child when the village is dysfunctional! Dysfunctional people will produce dysfunctional children.

The standard mode of ancient warfare was hand-to-hand combat, with nobody in front and nobody to cover your back. This became increasingly difficult and antiquated as technology and militaristic maneuverings began to advance. Hand-to-hand combat diminished in popularity for war when modern-day weaponry made it easier to fight your enemy from afar: never seeing their eyes. Something has happened, we now we want to fight our battles without ever facing them. However, when the Lord puts you in the trenches, you cannot avoid your battle. He makes you face the very thing that is trying to destroy you. Not because He is sadistic, but because He knows that you will never be more than a conqueror until you have the stamina to look your enemy in the eye. That thing that has been trying to dismantle you; the issue that has been trying to uproot your family; the thoughts that have been warring with your conscience, your self-esteem, your identity, and attacking your purpose, is the very thing you should face head-on. Be strong in your conviction that God is mighty in battle and He is on your side.

The soldier who feels he has no support or that he is in the battleground alone is more prone to self-distraction because he is quicker to retreat. So in military lines, they send the most zealous to front lines, put the most experienced in the back lines, and everybody else in the middle. Those that were zealous but lacked experience, would see that there was a whole army behind them, if ever they wanted to turn tail and run. Those who were in the middle of the tenure, not sure whether to press forward or move backward, could look in either direction and know that there was somebody surrounding them. The more experienced warriors would cheer on those at the front line saying, "I remember when I was in that position."

> *When the Lord puts you in the trenches, you cannot avoid your battle. He makes you face the very thing that is trying to destroy you.*

Can you imagine how much more healthy the body of Christ would be if we knew those who more seasoned Christians were backing them who were just arriving at the battle? What seems to have happened though, is that civil war in the body of Christ has broken ranks. Those who are veterans in the kingdom seemingly want to wipe out and assassinate those new to the uniform. God is saying, *"If you have had some scars, please do not downplay those who just got through basic training. Show them how you were able to survive. Show them how you were able to persevere. Because you were not always the soldier you are now and there were moments when you made mistakes, had some misfires and lost your aim. Somebody was there backing you and cheering you on."*

---★---

The devil wants to fool you into believing that when you are going through a battle you are going through it by yourself

---★---

Then there are those of us who are in the middle section that have not been saved a long time but weren't saved just yesterday either. And every time we thought about going back home, every time we thought about quitting, every time we thought about throwing down our weapons, we realized that the Bible was true. Don't you know that you are surrounded by a great cloud of witnesses? You need to know that wherever you are, there is somebody in front of you or somebody behind you who has been through the situation you are facing or is in it right now.

The enemy wants to divide and conquer us. The devil wants to fool you into believing that when you are going through a battle you are going through it by yourself, but the reason you attend church is so you will have fellowship. This is the basic principle of understanding: I am not the only fellow on the ship, but there is somebody else who is going through the same crisis that I am in the midst of. Don't think you are the only one who is financially broke, that you have the only messed-up marriage, or that yours is the only child running wild, or that you alone are battling depression. Every time you attend church, *don't* think of it as visiting a museum, but a hospital; because everybody there has issues they are dealing with. The good news is, you and I are destined to win.

In warfare, the enemy's plot is always to segment soldiers so they feel isolated, vulnerable, and alone. In Aesop's fable about the lion and the three oxen, the lion wanted to devour the three oxen but could not because they all stuck together. The lion devised a plan to turn the oxen against one another so he could eat them one at a time. He began to pour seeds of dissension so that one ox became jealous of another. They didn't realize they were playing into the trap of their enemy. They didn't have sense enough to understand that as long as they stuck together they would always have success. Children of God, understand if there is anywhere in the world where there should **not** be jealousy, envy, and backbiting, it's in the house of God. If all of us would come to understand the importance of unity among the brethren, then no weapon formed against us would be able to prosper. The problem is that we get too concerned about who has what, who is driving what, and who is living where. We ought to understand that all of us are under attack, and it is not until we fight *for* one another that we as the body of Christ will be able to win.

You were born to fight not only your own, but also somebody else's battles. In other words, God created you with someone else's battle in mind. So the heartaches that you have experienced in your life was not all for you. But God was taking you through basic training so that because of your experience, somebody coming behind you wouldn't die on the battleground. You may never even get to know how many lives you've saved by your witness, your testimony, or just by showing up.

> *You were born to fight not only your own, but also somebody else's battles.*

You were born for this. You were created not only to be blessed, but also to go into battle so that somebody other than you may be blessed. There is somebody whose life is waiting to see if you are going to come to church and look good, or if you are going to arrive, roll up your sleeves and fight for someone else's victory. From the Word of God, we know that a brother is born for adversity and a friend for hard times; so if you want to check out who your real friends are, find the people who don't like what you are facing, but aren't uncomfortable around you through it.

Friendship is about giving and receiving support, regardless of what is known about each other. Some people hate on you without even knowing what your real issues are. But when you can love somebody even when you know their mess, you know their life is a wreck, but you stand by them anyway, then and only then can you lay claim on the title *friend*. By God's standard, this is the kind of friend you should be looking out for, and to be. You were born not for comfort, you were born not for ease; rather, you were born to fight. Amazingly, you were not even born for your own fight. This is the reason four out of five times your phone rings, someone needs something, and you catch yourself wondering why they keep calling you. Of course you have problems of your own, but that's God giving you a wake-up call—a reminder that you were born to be a warrior. You bear an anointing so strong that not only will it fight your fight, but it can even take on somebody else's fight as well, and win both!

God is connecting you, not necessarily to someone who likes to fight, but to someone familiar with your fight who is not intimidated by your fight.

If you were born to battle for someone else's good and not just your own, then somewhere out there someone was born for your good. The problem is, you keep trying to fix everything on your own, forgetting that God has already orchestrated your victory. Somebody across town whom might never have met, you've not even shaken hands, but is being sent by God to be a blessing to you. It is not coincidence that you come in contact with the people you do on any given day. As a matter of fact, God woke some of them up just so they could be beside you, so that you would not have to fight by yourself.

God is connecting you, not necessarily to someone who likes to fight, but to someone familiar with your fight who is not intimidated by your fight. Whatever you are going through, they have gone through and know the terrain of that type of battleground. For this reason, when you are going through the worst time in your life, the most devastating thing you can do is to keep it to yourself. You've got to tell someone what you are going through because they might have an insight as to how you can overcome what you are dealing with. You may not have to tell everybody, but you certainly do need to tell somebody. The enemy wants you to act as if you are in the witness protection program, like you aren't going through anything and nothing is wrong in your life. But when you are bold enough to come into the house of the Lord and say, "I don't know what I am doing and Father, but if I've ever needed you before, I certainly need you now. I am not going to die, because I was born for this. Whatever I am going through right now, I was born to take on this fight and even so, to win." If the enemy had had his way, he would certainly have loved to kill you, but because God's plan for you is not for disaster, He has surrounded you with some folk that know this and keep you reminded that you are more than a conqueror.

In essence, your ministry is to bless the people who are connected to you. You probably don't even understand why you stress more over your friends' and family's issues than your own; but know that God has revealed to you what your assignment for ministry is. God puts them on your mind because he knows you've got the weapons needed to fight for them in the spirit realm. Whoever this may be—family, coworker, or simply friend—I dare you to fight with them and for them in the spiritual realm, saying, "This is not for me. This is for my brother/sister who is going through, my friend who is on the verge of giving up, or my family member who feels like they are only hanging on the tip of their rope." In other words, let somebody else benefit from your fight because God never blesses anyone so that they can exercise selfishness. If it benefits you alone then it is not a dream, but a goal.

> *Though one may be overpowered, two can defend themselves. A cord of three strands is not quickly broken.*
>
> —Ecclesiastes 4:12

The typical, traditional way to interpret this scripture is dealing with marriage. But let's look at that text with a warfare lens. See that what it is saying is not necessarily between a husband, a wife, and God; but it is saying that you've got to understand that the three cords that are intertwined together will not be broken. Because we are AME (African Methodist Episcopal), we ascribe to the Trinitarian theology. Trinitarians believe that there is a three-cord God-head with one dominion. We believe in God the Father, Son, and Holy Spirit. *"In the beginning was the Word and the Word was with God and the Word was God..."* (John 1:1). When looking at this verse alone, you read, *"In the beginning was God..."* Here, you are dealing with the identity of God. *And the Word was with God* deals with the personality of God. *"And the Word became flesh and dwelt among us..."* (John 1:14) deals with the deity of God. So when you are under attack, God says, "I have put three things in line for you. Your identity is will not be stripped, your personality won't be lost, and the spirit man in you will never be destroyed. In order for the enemy to kill you, he's got to get through three layers before he can even touch the core of who you are. He's got to get through your personality, your identity, and then your spirit, which he cannot break.

As Trinitarians, we believe in the tripod oneness of God; the Father, the Son, and the Holy Ghost. Jesus said that even though he was going away, He would send us the comforter. The comforter is the Holy Ghost. There are some seasons in life when it seems difficult to hear from God, but even when we have not heard from God, we know we can stand on God's Word, which assures us there is a friend that sticks closer than any brother. For all the times when you feel like you are alone, remember that there is too much going for you to be down-trodden. The comforter is with you.

Mark 2:1–12 gives us two different dynamics and dimensions of how the three different cords operate and function. There are three kinds of friends in this portion of scripture; a friend who is helpless, a friend who is helpful, and a friend who heals. There is a man who is sick of palsy and he can't get to Jesus because he is unable to walk. His limbs are incapacitated and he is helpless, but the Lord assigned him four friends who must have said amongst themselves, "Even though we can walk, we shall not be satisfied until he too can walk." They couldn't get to the door of the building where Jesus was, but they didn't give up. They said to one another, "Let's climb up and break up the roof, then we can lower our friend down." (paraphrased) You see, you don't need a whole army of friends. You just need a few people who will urge you on when you can't go the extra mile on your own. Sometimes you need to thank God even for the friends who seem to let you down, because things are not always what they seem to be. Much as they may not intend to, they could actually be taking you closer to Jesus.

Jesus, in the middle of His sermon, notices that He has to stop preaching because something is coming through the roof. When He looks up, He sees a man being lowered on a bed. Of course this man didn't get there by himself, but he has four friends up there who had enough audacity to tear the roof off the building which didn't even belong to them.

The four friends who helped him could walk and not anywhere in the Bible do we see the four friends as having issues or problems of their own. Sometimes God will bless you in situations you haven't even discussed, just because you made an effort to help somebody else. There is a default anointing you are bound to receive just because of all the people you have blessed along the way. God will to do something for you. Maybe they didn't appreciate you, maybe they didn't say thank you, or perhaps they didn't value you, but watch God bless you because you blessed someone else. You have got to find friends who are helpless and helpful, then find one friend who knows how to heal. If you ever get to a place where friends let you down, look around because they may have let you down right in the very place God wanted you to be all along.

I have learned to thank God for everybody who dropped me, because when they dropped me, they meant it for evil but God used it for my good. You ought to thank God for those who were your enemies as well as those who were your friends by accident because if they did not hurt you, you wouldn't know how to pray, you wouldn't know how to trust God, and you wouldn't know how to celebrate your victories.

> ★
>
> *You ought to thank God for those who were your enemies as well as those who were your friends by accident because if they did not hurt you, you wouldn't know how to pray*
>
> ★

The Lord has put you in a strategic position where the battle you are facing would not be all about you. Your fight is connected to four other people on top of the roof. In other words, when you come through this, there are four other people who are going to get blessed at the same time. There are four other people connected to the battle you are in right now. Four plus one is five, which is the number of favor. God grants favor as you surround yourself with the right kind of people. Even as you go through, say to yourself, "This fight is not bigger than I am; this fight is not greater than I am. I am so anointed that I can take it on, even for four other people. I was born for this!"

The battle we are fighting has nothing to do with tangible things, but it has everything to do with who you are in God and how God perceives you to be. Don't be overwhelmed by the battle you are in. If you don't get overwhelmed, you won't get overtaken. The battle is not yours, it is the Lord's.

I will never forget my junior year of college, I was without focus and discipline. I bought a 1979 Mercedes Benz. I was excited about it because I would be the only person on campus driving a Mercedes Benz. The car's owner lived next to the falling Berlin wall. He had to return home, and I met him the day he had to leave. He was selling the Benz for two thousand dollars, and that excited me. So here I was living on campus and driving a Mercedes Benz. I was the campus talk: "Jamal Bryant is driving a Mercedes Benz."

It didn't matter to me what model year the Benz was or what mileage it had. Two weeks later I sped through a stop sign and was immediately pulled over by the police who wanted to know who I was because I was. I was too short to be a basketball player, too skinny to be a football player, and not wearing enough gold to be a rap artist. This was my first car, and I didn't know what owning a car entailed. The police officer asked for my title and insurance. Of course the title wasn't in my name and the car had no insurance. Immediately, I was locked up.

I was the son of a bishop, getting ready to graduate, I was a chapel assistant and the president of the local chapter of the NAACP, and here I was, in jail and charged for stolen tags and a stolen car. The only person who could verify that the car belonged to me was overseas, and I didn't have a number to reach him. At the time, not many people knew who I was. I was stranded. My parents were living in Africa, and my friends were fellow college students who couldn't afford three thousand dollars to bail me out. I was very scared, especially after all the stories I had heard about what goes on in prison cells.

> ★
>
> *Everybody in jail looked at me because at that time I was twenty-two years old and they all assumed I was a drug dealer.*
>
> ★

After ten minutes in prison, the jail keeper came, asking, "Is there a Jamal Bryant in here?"

I scampered to my feet and said, "Yes, it's me." In my spirit I was thinking someone anonymous must have paid the bail.

He said, "Mr. Bryant, are you the owner of the blue Mercedes Benz with white leather interior and white wheel tires?"

I answered, "Yes it's me."

He said, "We just want you to know that your car has been impounded but it's safe." Everybody in jail looked at me because at that time I was twenty-two years old and they all assumed I was a drug dealer. I was surrounded by pedophiles, murderers, and rapists.

One by one they came to me saying, "Man, look out for me when you get out. Can you give me a job?"

Immediately, by instinct, I wanted to tell them the truth. *"No I am not a drug dealer. I am a stupid college student who bought a car that doesn't match my present status."*

But the Lord immediately whispered to me, *"Be cool, and don't be overwhelmed. You are going to get out of this."*

The lesson I learned is that sometimes people will think you are what you are not, and it's that assumption that will get you out in the end. The most valuable lesson I learned was that sometimes you can be in the wrong place doing the right thing, without the right paperwork, but because you stand with God, you do not have to say anything. Your mistakes will turn out to be the platform for a miracle.

★

Sometimes people will think you are what you are not, and it's that assumption that will get you out in the end.

★

Three days later, all of my friends on campus pulled money together to bail me out. This gave me a story to tell. They believed the only way you could drive a good car is by doing something illegal. It wasn't until I went to jail that I had the chance to witness that I didn't do anything illegal, but was just previewing what God was about to do.

Ten years later, I was driving a Bentley, and people were still trying to figure out whether I was a basketball player, football player, or a rap artist. What is even more amazing, however, is that now drug dealers go to my church, and I have to let them know that I am able to do what I do, not because I did something illegal, but because I did something that stretched me out in faith ten years ago, while I was still in college. *I had a Mercedes vision!* God had to elevate me. If He could give me a Mercedes Benz in college, how much more will He give me now that I am sold out to him? I had to learn not to be so overwhelmed.

> *I was born to be a pastor, teacher, father, and husband, however, I was dying because I was living as something else.*

The prisoners asked me whether I was a basketball player or a drug dealer. I should have told, "I was born to be a preacher." Little did I know I was trying to live up to an image that put me in jail. What I was born to do I denied and ended up in prison. God was me a warning me at the time. I did not understand until now. Being locked into an image had the potential of incarcerating my destiny. There is a popular book entitled, *You Were Born an Original, Don't Die a Copy.* I was born to be a pastor, teacher, father, and husband, however, I was dying because I was living as something else.

Chapter 6

I'VE BEEN HIT

———————★———————

"The hardest hit is the one you never see coming."
— Anonymous

Not too long ago, the largest newspaper in our area called my office and asked to do an in-depth article on us. Our church had grown at a miraculous rate, and we were becoming both a spiritual and political force in the community. They conducted extensive interviews with people who had known me a long time— people who mentored me, church members, family, friends, and even political figures in the community. All of them were asked about the influence Empowerment Temple had on the city of Baltimore. Little did I know that it was going to make the front page of the Sunday edition of *The Baltimore Sun,* the most widely circulated, widely read, widely discussed edition of the paper.

The Sunday morning that article appeared, I was headed to church for the first of our three morning services. My phone exploded with calls.

"Jamal, you are not going to believe it. There is a large picture of you on the front page of *The Baltimore Sun* newspaper. The article is called 'Rich in Spirit.'"

Though I had no idea the story was going to run in the Sunday edition, and I was very glad for the exposure. With the hard work of numerous dedicated staff members and church volunteers, our congregation experienced phenomenal growth. We were doing what God had called us to do—bringing life to those who'd given up on God—and God was prospering us in that work. I also took some personal delight in knowing that some of my detractors would be in a rage over that story. There I was on the front page of the paper. I wasn't a football player, a law breaker, or an entertainer. I was just trying to help people through ministry. Now here I was on the front page of the widely read Baltimore Sun.

When I arrived at the church, I went to my office. The place had an eerie feel, it was so quiet. Everyone was going about their usual business, but no one talked. In my office, I found the newspaper spread across my desk. I sat down to read it with tremendous excitement, eager to see how the newspaper was championed our cause. As I read, my smile turned into a frown.

Much to my dismay, the reporter painted me as a prosperity preacher. The article talked about the cars I drove, the house I lived in, and the clothes I wore. It placed more emphasis on those outward appearances than on what our ministry was doing to empower and equip people. By the time I finished reading, I was in a fit.

The story never mentioned how many people we'd rescued people from homeless despair or of Tuesday Bible study when every person has a ride home, or how we give away clothes twice a year to mothers and to people who are being released from prison. I had been hit. I was afraid to go out and face my congregation. I wondered how they would react when we reached the point in the service where we collected the offering. What would they think of me? Would I appear to them as attempting to fill my own coffers? Would they feel prostituted for my benefit?

Of all days for that article to appear, that particular Sunday was "Stewardship Sunday". I was slated to preach about tithes, offerings, and first-fruits and the importance of giving back to God.

I did it, but I was certain our members were saying in their hearts, *"He's going to use our tithe money to buy another suit. He's going to use my seed money to refurbish his home. He's going to use my offering to buy another car."*

At first I thought it was just a suckerpunch, then I realized the enemy had declared war. We had to fight back.

The American homeland has been attacked twice since the War of 1812. Once at Pearl Harbor and then with the attacks of September 11, 2001. When the terrorists flew those airplanes into the World Trade Center in New York that Tuesday morning, they were not attacking haphazardly but with a systematic process. They didn't crash those planes into whichever buildings they saw first, randomly choosing targets as they went. They had three carefully chosen, predetermined objectives in mind.

---★---

When the terrorists flew those airplanes into the World Trade Center in New York that Tuesday morning, they were not attacking haphazardly but with a systematic process.

---★---

The first of those targets was the World Trade Center. This was strategic because the World Trade Center was the symbolic center of the American economy and a crucial link in the global financial industry. Many international transactions were cleared through facilities in those buildings.

The second place they struck was the Pentagon. Recognized around the world, that five-sided structure housed more office space than any office building in the world. More than that, it was the symbol of American military might and security.

The third target was the White House. Symbolically the heart of American political leadership, that building represented more than just the presidency. Much like the national flag, that building represented the heart of the entire country and the heart of its people.

When the enemy hits you in those three areas (finance, security, and leadership) you know he's coming in an all-out attack. He is coming to destroy the things on which you thought you could always rely. Things you once thought were untouchable. Things you were sure would never be vulnerable to attack.

When you are anointed by God and living under attack, the first thing that starts to go is your finances. In an attack, money issues come to the front. You might be earning more money than ever before, but in a season of attack you'll be broke all the time. You tithe and watch your expenses, but you still struggle.

> *When you are anointed by God and living under attack, the first thing that starts to go is your finances.*

Right after your money is attacked, your security takes a hit. Part of this issue is tied up in the fact that we often claim to trust God but what we are really trusting is our bank account. You work hard, making good money. Maybe your spouse and you both work, and income isn't normally an issue. It's very easy to think you are trusting God when, in fact, you are relying on that bank account. When someone asks for a hundred dollars, it's easy to give it to them if you have thousands in an account. The real test comes when you only have a hundred in the bank.

A challenge to your security can come as an internal attack. It can also come as an external attack. People you used to be able to count on and depend on walk away. Often those are people to whom you've been close for years.

When your finances have been hit and your security is in jeopardy, the enemy comes after the leadership. People you relied upon for advice and guidance are no longer available. Good voices become hard to find.

> *Satan only attacks people who are going somewhere. Whenever he attacks you, it's a clear indication that you are moving in the correct direction.*

When they put Jesus on the cross that Friday afternoon, the first thing they did was nail His hands. Hands are a metaphor for work, productivity, and creativity.

When God anoints you, He anoints you with creative imagination. You start to see how things can be done in a different way. You have new and fresh ideas. Creativity is unleashed. The enemy attacks by going after that creativity. An attack like that often comes at your place of employment.

An attack on your creativity will look very much like the final attack on Jesus. The people at work you thought were your friends will be the very ones who have set you up for failure and planned your demise. Your closest coworkers will be the ones looking to betray you. In the mornings, you'll find yourself stressed before you make it to the car to leave for work. The thought of another day in battle will leave you drained and spent. After a while, you won't feel like getting out of bed. The money they pay you won't be worth the pain you go through each day on the job. You're being crucified, and your job is being crucified because Satan is out to kill, steal, and destroy your creativity.

After they nailed Jesus' hands, they nailed His feet. Feet serve as a metaphor for progress or movement. Satan only attacks people who are going somewhere. Whenever he attacks you, it's a clear indication that you are moving in the correct direction. You are leaning into your gift, learning to operate in the strength of God's unique expression of His presence in your life. That keeps you moving toward your destiny. Satan doesn't like that. He will do his best to stop you from getting to the next level. He doesn't want you to see more of the manifestation of your gift. As I told you earlier, any move toward God meets with opposition from Satan. As long as he's opposing you, you know you're doing something right.

After the Romans nailed Jesus' hands and feet to the cross, they hoisted him in place. Sometime later, they pierced His side. The side of a man's body is the place beneath his arm. It is a place of vulnerability. It is also the place from which God took a rib and made woman from man. I know all the feminists will read that and be upset. Don't be. It doesn't mean anything about dominance. The fact that Eve is portrayed as coming from Adam's side indicates that man's side is a place of intimacy and vulnerability.

There is no pain like the pain of being hurt by someone close to you. People whom you never expected to turn on you have now done so. Like a quarterback on the football field, you've been hit from the blind side, the side opposite your throwing hand—an attack so unexpected you never saw it coming.

Attacks like that drain you. They leave you without the energy to cry and so mad you're numb, especially when you've been wounded by your own friends, your family, someone who had your confidence and with whom you let down your guard.

Before they nailed Jesus on the cross, lifted him in place, and pierced His side, they put a crown of thorns on His head. Not a real crown, but one made to mock His claim of authority. (Matthew 27:27-31; Mark 15:16-20; John 19:1-5)

When you think nothing else can happen to you, and when those who attack you seem to have the upper hand and the damage has been done, they turn to the most debilitating, humiliating form of mockery they can conceive. Something that totally misrepresents you, yet gives a hint of fact and makes it hard to refute. An attack like that leaves you on the verge of losing control. Don't.

After the cross, after the mockery, after the humiliation, comes the resurrection. If you break loose at any of those points and go after your attacker to destroy them, you will lose your resurrection. At a moment like this, it's easy to think about doing things you wouldn't ordinarily do. This is where all that discipline and self-control we talked about earlier really comes into play. Sit tight. Help is on the way.

Friday was bad, but Sunday's coming. Death looks dark, but the resurrection is a glorious thing to behold. God will work a resurrection in your circumstances.

The enemy attacks you at work to get to your creativity. He attacks your finances to reach your security. He attacks your leadership to slow you down and hinder your progress. He doesn't attack with strangers—he uses people you know. That's because God is getting ready to shift you to a new position. You've come to a transition point in life. It looks like a hit. It hurts like a hit. Satan and the people who've attacked you think it's a hit. The real problem is the people around you cannot handle the level of greatness to which you are about to ascend. God has to move them out to move you up.

The real problem is the people around you cannot handle the level of greatness to which you are about to ascend. God has to move them out to move you up.

When God starts showing you things that don't relate to your present-day reality, things you've never seen before, things you've never known before, you'd better check your armor. Pull that chinstrap tighter on your helmet. Sharpen the edge of your sword. The enemy will be coming after you. He doesn't want you learning anything new. He doesn't want you moving up to the next level. Expect an attack at any moment.

There are three reasons why you are under attack. The first is because of spiritual growth. When you get to a place where you know you are growing spiritually, expect an attack. You are not the same person you used to be. Transformation is at work in your life. God is moving you from one thing to the next. Old habits are dropping away. New ones are forming. The enemy opposes every move toward God.

The second reason the enemy will attacks is because you are invading his territory. The enemy has no problem with those who contain their faith and confine it to mere religious practice. But when you start testifying at work, you become a target. Those who simply show up in church for the Easter service are not a threat to the kingdom of darkness. But when you start going to people with whom you used to commit all manner of sin, and you don't allow them to compromise you but instead raise them to your level, watch out. You've invaded enemy territory. When you say to your community, "We aren't harboring drug dealers anymore." When you say to your community, "It's time that everyone had access to the means by which they can achieve their destiny." When you move out of the pews and down to the street corners and offer people life, then you've invaded the enemy's territory. If you weren't engaged in battle before you did all of that, you certainly will be afterward.

The third reason you are under attack is because the enemy senses what is coming in your life. He isn't omniscient or omnipresent. He doesn't know everything, and he isn't everywhere at once. He can't see the future, but he is crafty, wily, and knows the spirit world very well. He can sense a move of God, and he does everything he can to cut it off.

When the attack on you intensifies, then you know the blessing is getting closer.

That article in *The Baltimore Sun* hit me hard. I never saw it coming. The reporter took me in and led me down a path; I had no idea an ambush was awaiting me. I made it through that Sunday, and many Sundays since. Some people didn't like me because of what they read. A lot more didn't like *The Baltimore Sun* for the article they published. Most people who knew me already knew how I dressed, what kind of car I drove, and where I lived. Nothing we do at Empowerment Temple has been done in the secret. Everything is right there in the open for all to see.

God doesn't work in a vacuum. He works in a context. The context at Empowerment Temple might not fit in the stereotypical church model. I hope it doesn't. God didn't call us to be the typical, hidebound, confined, ineffective church we see so much of today. A church style that works in south Alabama won't work in Baltimore. One that works in a white community, a Hispanic community, or a Chinese community won't be relevant to a black community. We are the church we are because of where we are, to reach the people to whom God has called us.

> ★
>
> *When you take a hit from the enemy, remind yourself of your calling. Not the calling everyone wants to put on you, but the calling God put on you.*
>
> ★

When you take a hit from the enemy, remind yourself of your calling. Not the calling everyone wants to put on you, but the calling God put on you. The one that got you started in the first place. You don't have to be like me. In fact, you shouldn't be like me. You should be like you. God made you one of a kind for the unique call and the distinct place He has for you. When you take a hit, remind yourself of just how special you are to God and how privileged you are to be in His service.

Many people over-estimate the power of the enemy. They believe immaturely that Satan is the ultra-equal of God. They believe he has the same knowledge, strength, and power. This isn't true. The enemy has limited power, authority, and information. Whenever you are under attack, usually it's with more than one thing at a time. Many things are thrown on your plate and your enemy waits to see which one you will respond to. The one you select will become the one on which he will focus. What I discovered later is once you have been hit, keep your guard up because more punches are on the way.

Chapter 7

DEALING WITH PRESSURE

★

A wise man has great power and a man of knowledge increases strength.

—Proverbs 24:5

Joseph Rudyard Kipling came up from the rough side of the mountain. He was starved of attention and affection. He was given up for adoption by his own parents and even while he was under the auspices of foster care found himself victimized by physical abuse. In spite of all the things he went through as a child, he was still able to gain the Nobel Prize in literature. He turned down the honor given him by the Queen for knighthood. and as he probed and reflected over his life; how it was that he was able to gain the stature he had, he sat down in 1908 and wrote a poem entitled "**If.**"

If you can keep your head when all about you
Are losing theirs and blaming it on you;
If you can trust yourself when all men doubt you,
But make allowance for their doubting too;
If you can wait and not be tired by waiting,
Or being lied about, don't deal in lies,
Or being hated, don't give way to hating,
And yet don't look too good, nor talk to wise:
If you can dream—and not make dreams your master;
If you can think—and not make thoughts your aim;
If you can meet with Triumph and Disaster
And treat those two imposters just the same;
If you can bear to hear the truth you've spoken
Twisted by knaves to make a trap for fools,
Or watch the things you gave your life to, broken,
And stoop and build 'em up with worn-out tools;
If you can make one heap of all your winnings
And risk it on one turn of pitch-and-toss,
And lose, and start again at your beginnings
And never breathe a waord about your loss;
If you can force your heart and nerve and sinew
To serve your turn long after they are gone,
And so hold on when there is nothing in you
Except the Will which says to them, "Hold on!"
If you can talk with crowds and keep your virtue,
Or walk with kings—nor lose the common touch,
If neither foes nor loving friends can hurt you,
If all men count with you, but none too much;
If you can fill the unforgiving minute
With sixty seconds' worth of distant run—
Yours is the earth and everything that's in it,
And—which is more—you'll be a Man my son.

   (Joseph Rudyard Kipling)

His whole focus and aim was to understand that in this raging warfare it doesn't even matter what kind of arsenal or technology you have for or against you. What is going to help you win is if you can keep your head. It's important that you learn to keep your emotions intact. You must learn to control them, rather than allowing them to dictate to you what you feel. Often-times the enemy will manipulate our emotions in order that we lose control, but we should make every effort to keep our wits about us and know that everything attacking in our emotions is designed to cause us to forget who we are in Christ; thus, losing our objectivity.

It wasn't until Vietnam that it was in fact understood that the greatest casualty of warfare was not physical psychological damage. So many of our fathers, grandfathers, brothers and uncles came dealing with the psychological trauma of warfare even while their bodies were still intact. One Vietnam veteran said, "It is almost as though we are living in a bad car accident day after day and even so, without the ambulance ever showing up."

> *What is going to help you win is if you can keep your head.*

In dealing with the stress and the trauma of going through warfare, please remember that there is no way you can go through war and not be psychologically impacted and affected. Everything you have gone through in life has made a deposit, affecting how you think and how you respond to different situations. And so while you might not have physical bruises or wounds, in your mind there is something that has assaulted you. Defenses are raised to prevent that kind of pain, or those types of injury from ever being inflicted again. Now you guard yourself, emotionally and mentally, not based on what you are presently going through, but on your memories of previous wounds. Many of us have been unable to have healthy relationships. The present relationship may have tremendous potential, but due to past hurts, failures,

Everything you have gone through in life has made a deposit, affecting how you think and how you respond to different situations.

or other emotional trauma, you are paralyzed, relationally. And because you still bear those wounds, you are unable to trust, love, believe, or be transparent because you were wounded in the last battle. Somehow your psyche clings to the previous struggles, disallowing you the revelation that your present situation is not the one in which you were entangled before. There's often a subtle impulse that carries the woes of the old over into the new.

Psychologists have deduced that after going through traumatic warfare, there is something called combat stress reaction, which is a mental state induced by combat that impairs the emotional, intellectual, and psychological ability of any soldier. There are people all around us, some closer than we realize, who have endured battles they've never talked about. Someone I know within our community has come through some pretty tough trials that are still wearing on them; they still bear the battle scars, though invisible to the eye, they are always present in the heart and mind.

Another attribute combat stress reaction is aggression and irritability. Quite often, after coming through fierce battles, the warrior's coping mechanism doesn't shut off and they become overly aggressive. The hostility isn't constantly directed toward an enemy any longer, but toward those closest to them, usually a spouse or children. They begin to lash out at whoever happens to be in their path. Those being hurt now are people who have never afflicted their abuser or done them ill. The aggressor has been wounded and taking their pain out on others. One trigger could be that they've had a rough day at work; they come home and take it out on everybody who's living in their house.

Not only is there aggression, but with depression. You feel a deep sense of self-criticism; with pessimism. These people can't see how the future will be any brighter than their past. After having gone through that kind of stress reaction, they don't have hope, they see everything as dismal around them. With such people, whenever good news is shared, they look for the hovering storm cloud. When something good happens in their lives, they tell themselves it's too good to be true.

Depression aside, there are others who deal with anxiety disorder. They are anxious about everything and can't be at peace or calm their spirit. They have trouble sleeping, focusing, and being at rest, because they are always in the kung-fu stance—ready to fight. They constantly assess your actions and words, looking for hidden meanings, innuendos, or gestures meant as an assault against them. They're wounded, expecting you to wound them further, creating an attitude of distrust in them toward you.

Some develop eating disorders. Whether eating too much or too little has nothing to do with hunger in these cases. The core issue is the person's inability to assuage the frayed nerves, tormenting thoughts, eating at them from the inside. If not through an eating disorder, they will look for an outlet in drug and/or alcohol abuse. They're desperate to drown away the tears, pain, and memory of the battle that has physically ended, but psychologically still rages on. If not that, then they will go through unbridled rage and anger triggered by virtually anything that upsets them—either the dinner is too hot or too cold, the TV or the children are too loud, the radio is on too much, or the computer doesn't cooperate. The list could go on. They become upset because they suffer from a wounded soul. It won't matter whether others are jumping to their feet or sitting, moving to the side or standing still. The anger of these wounded refuses to be pacified. They're bothered, whatever anyone does to make things better. They're disturbed by the person driving slowly in front of them. Psychologically, they're convinced that the pain they feel is coming from outside forces and not from within.

What do we do with that kind of disorder? How do we deal with the afflictions of combat stress reaction? This phenomenon has a spiritual dimension to it too. There are a lot of people who sit in church and have gone through combat stress reaction, evidenced by their immediate memory loss. They've forgotten that God fought battles for them in the past. If God was there in the past, what is there that indicates He won't be there to fight for you in the future? We don't dare forget, this is not the first time money has been scarce, it is not the first time anyone's been in a dysfunctional relationship, it is not the first time anyone's child rebelled, this isn't the first time there's been a lack of transportation. If God brought you through the last time, you've got to have faith and confidence that He will do it again!

> *If God brought you through the last time, you've got to have faith and confidence that He will do it again!*

In order to know where your tolerance lie in a stressful situation, have those you trust as mentors place you in situations and circumstances where you must deal with the pressure. You'll see soon whether you can handle it.

In order to be selected among the elite troops, you must endure trials that other people don't have to experience. It's important for you to understand that the reason your tribulations are much more intense than those around you is because the Lord has handpicked you to be a part of His elite force. There is something He has built into your character that give strength to endure when others would break under the pressure. Do you want to know how anointed you are? Look at all that you've been through without losing your integrity or your testimony. Look at the intense situations you've suffered through without the assistance of a psychotherapist. God has protected you. He has allowed you to go through certain situations to strengthen you and show you whether you can handle pressure or if you would break down over simple situations.

─────────★ ─────────

In the Navy, recruits go through hell week. You have to persevere through hell week in order to become a Navy SEAL.

─────────★ ─────────

In the Navy, recruits go through hell week. You have to persevere through hell week in order to become a Navy SEAL. During the last part of "hell week", they make you drown-proof. They tie your arms and your feet, and then throw you in a swimming pool. You've got to learn then how to float in the water for twenty minutes with your hands tied and your feet bound but still keep yourself above water. After you do this, you move to the next phase of the exercise. Next, you've got to go underwater for ten minutes with your hands tied, your legs bound, and still not lose your head. Passed? It's still not the end... After you rise to the surface again; you are now required to swim for a hundred feet, with your hands bound, your feet tied and still maintain a level head.

There are times when the enemy has put me under great pressure, but what the enemy didn't understand was that putting me under pressure as he had, he didn't have to worry about tying up my hands and tying up my feet. What he should have done was to seal my mouth because when my back was up against the wall, I could still fight my way through. You probably remember some situations in your own life where the circumstances of life had your hands tied and your feet bound, but you still learned how to swim out of the thorny situations. You learned to swim when under tremendous pressure and pushed through the resistance, even when you thought drowning was imminent.

When you come through "hell week" successfully, the Navy gives you a seal that indicates you are drown-proof. No matter what life deals you, you'll still going to rise to the top because the Lord has tested you.

There was a man by the name of Lazarus who was dead and in the grave. Mary and Martha said to Jesus, it is too late. There is no way he is going to come out of this situation alive, but Jesus said, "Show me where you laid him." They said, "Jesus, by now his body stinks." The Lord ignored that and said, "Roll the stone away." And the Lord went to the edge of the grave and said, "Lazarus, come forth." And Lazarus came jumping out with his hands tied and his feet bound. Everybody had written him off as dead and gone— until Jesus came on the scene (John 11 *paraphrased)*. You are not dead. Jesus just hasn't called your name yet. The interesting thing about Lazarus is that he could come out jumping even when he was in a bind. It's easy to shout when there's nothing on you, but can you praise God with the weight of the world on your shoulders?

The Navy takes each shipmen through these tests to see if they are equipped for the elite squad. The lesson to learn is that you have got to be motivated and determined to never give up, even when you are incapacitated. There is something about you that pleases God. He knows that when times are tough, you don't punk out, you don't start crying, you don't get riled, angry or bitter. Pity parties are rare because you understand whose you are. If you weep or cry, it's due to the pain in the situation, however, you know that God is faithful. There's enough determination in you that says, "I am not going to die in the middle of this because the Lord is not finished with me yet. I may not be the greatest success, but one thing is true: I'm determined. I don't have it all together yet, but I'm determined."

In dealing with militaristic strategy it is incumbent upon the trainer to tell the recruits to know their position. Through statistical data it was found that when soldiers are in a bunker, they have to be recalibrated to understand their position. Whether they are in a bunker or a dugout, they have to understand they are not in a hiding position. Rather, they are in a fighting position. They are underground. The enemy can't see them, but they can see the enemy. Some people have misunderstood your posture. They think you are scared and hiding out but they don't understand that right now God has you positioned. So many people don't recognize your greatness, but God says, "It's not time for you to rise up yet." Basically He's saying, "I just need you to stay in the cut for a minute because when I introduce you to the world, people will want to know where you have been all this time with all that anointing on your life." They're all going to know you.

In order for you to win, you've got to be in the right fighting position. A military strategist out of the Pentagon says, in order to win, the soldier has got to be in the right posture. If the soldier is slumped over with his head down then his body has been taken over by the spirit of defeat, but if a soldier has his shoulders squared and his head lifted, anybody seeing him knows he is trained for battle. You cannot go to church looking like your situation. You've got to start going to church looking like your destiny. How is your financial situation? Don't show up advertising that you're destitute. Square your shoulders, walk with confidence, God is your provider. Is your heart broken? Walk into church wearing a smile. If the joy of the Lord is your strength tell your countenance!

Your body has got to be in the right posture in the right position because according to physiologists, your mind takes counsel after the posture of the body. So your body sends signals to your mind of what it is it should be prepared for. So you have to understand your praise is militaristic. Whenever you see me praising God, don't think that everything is right in my life. I am praising God because I am sending a signal to my mind to get ready because we are getting out of this. We are ready to fight our way through. In other words, when I praise Him, it is not based on how I feel. I praise Him based on who He is. The psalmist says to "delight yourself in the Lord and He will give you the desires of your heart. (Psalm

85

37:4) If you want nothing from God, then maybe you do not have to praise Him, but if you believe God is a good father and will open up a window and pour you down a blessing, the likes of which you can't contain, then take your position. You are assigned to get on the frontline, so you've got to let the enemy know you are entering his camp and you are not leaving until you reclaim what's yours.

★

You are assigned to get on the frontline, so you've got to let the enemy know you are entering his camp and you are not leaving until you reclaim what's yours.

★

When a soldier is holding his position, what the enemy doesn't understand is that the soldier is under pressure but not unprepared. No matter what happens, he can handle it. I am prepared to get lose my job, I am prepared for you to leave me, I am prepared for you to talk about me because I have been built for the struggle, and I am growing stronger every day. In the midst of the intense pressure you are under, God says, "I have allowed this pressure to come because I am preparing to build you so that tribulations that would have broken you last year cannot faze you this year; because you have been built to withstand the pressure."

The Air Force has something akin to the Navy "hell week". In the Air Force they understand that the best soldier will only be best prepared to fight if he is in a circumstance that appears real. You really don't know what a soldier is made of unless he is in a situation that requires him to use his skill. And when he is in the real situation, then his character will become evident. So during their equivalent of the "hell week" they get their highest cadets and put them in separate planes. Once the aircraft reaches forty thousand feet, they simulate an impending crash. They force the craft into a nose dive then they hand out sheets of paper instructing everyone, "You are going to die in probably two minutes so just in case your family finds this, write down in one word what you want. You may not survive it but while the plane is going down, write down what you expect to happen in case you do." What the cadet needs to remember, while the plane is going down, is that he's got a parachute on his back. Even if the plane doesn't make it, he can still jump and make it.

If nobody else around you survives, you've got to make up in your mind that you will. So even when your plane in life seems to be crashing, make sure you've got the parachute of faith. The rest can sit down and look at you funny if they want, but you have got to jump and live.

Just before the plane hits the ground, the trainers take the plane back up. They want to gauge whether the cadets were shocked at their near death experience or excited they are still alive. You can probably recall some situations that could have crushed you in the past year, but God redirected the course of events just in the nick of time and you are still here.

There is a special anointing that God is imparting to a special "elite" who know how to handle pressure. This is why

God has preserved you even throughout all the pressure you have been under.

We live in a time when we are bombarded with reality shows: *The $25 Million Dollar Hoax, 30 Seconds of Fame, The Amazing Race, American Idol, America's Next Top Model, Anything for Love, The Apprentice, The Bachelor, Big Brother, The Biggest Loser, Deal or No Deal, Dancing with the Stars, Extreme Makeover, Fear Factor, Project Runway, The Simple Life, Skating with Celebrities, So You Think You Can Dance, Survivor, The Weakest Link,* and the list goes on. Out of the numerous shows, however, the one that grabbed my attention was called *The Contender* produced by Mark Burnett and hosted by former boxer Sugar Ray Leonard. The show follows a group of boxers as they compete for a championship prize title and how their families fare alongside them. In one show, one of the underdog boxers said something that captivated my attention: "I am not the strongest, I am not the tallest, I am not the one most courageous, but the thing that puts me above everybody else is that I have a mind of a champion! Other people get in the ring, get frustrated, and lose the fight, but I keep my mind focused. Even though my opponent is bigger than I am, even though he is stronger and taller than I am, I remind myself that if I win over my mind I will win over his body." This is the testament over emotional discipline. So many people do not have the heart. The Lord wants us to have the heart to fight. It is not enough to simply show up with our body. The emotional discipline we ought to have should help us override temptation when we see it coming.

After his baptism, Jesus was led by the Spirit into a neighboring wilderness. The purpose was that he might be "tempted of the devil." Jesus Christ was tempted by the Devil throughout his ministry. Hebrews 4:15 says, ...*but we have one who has been tempted in every way, just as we are—yet was without sin.* The temptations of Jesus were real. Hebrews 2:18 says, *Because He Himself suffered when He was tempted, He is able to help those who are being tempted.* From the temptations of Jesus in Matthew 4:1–11, we can learn two important things: First, to know the process of temptation, and second, how to overcome temptation.

> *Then was Jesus led up by the Spirit into the desert to be tempted by the devil. After fasting forty days and forty nights, He was hungry. The tempter came to Him and said, 'If you are the Son of God, tell these stones become bread.*
>
> —Matthew 4:1–3

The first temptation was at the level of His physical nature, to turn stones to bread. He was hungry and the devil gave him a suggestion of what to do. The devil tempted Jesus through his human physical wishes, in the same way that Adam and Eve were tempted. As leaders, we get tempted too, but we need to walk through our lives and find out those emotional disciplines we ought to have– similar to what Jesus had. For Jesus, God's will was more important than the satisfaction of His hunger. Every day the devil brings doubts before us regarding our physical needs, but we ought to trust that Jehovah Jireh–our provider–is not in a crisis. He will not hide from the essence of His own nature. In fact, when you know for sure who you are in Christ, you have no need to prove it. Jesus answered and said, *"It is written: Man does not live on bread alone, but on every word that comes from the mouth of God."*

> *Then the devil took Him up into the holy city, and had Him stand on the highest point of the temple. 'If you are the Son of God,' he said, 'throw yourself down. For it is written: 'He will command His angels concerning you, and they will lift you up in their hands, so that you will not strike your foot against a stone.' Jesus answered him: "It is written: 'Do not put the Lord your God to the test.'"*

—Matthew 4:5-7

The second temptation was at the level of His spiritual nature to prove His faith in God. Jesus was not willing to depart from the will of God in the spiritual realm either. So, again, He depended and believed in the Word of God. When we reject the Word of God and do not trust and depend on it, we will fail for sure. Adam and Eve failed because they did not keep and trust the Word of God. But when we stick to it as we ought, then it will uphold us in our time of battle.

> *Again, the devil took Him up to a a very high mountain and showed Him all the kingdoms of the world and their splendor. "All this things I will give you," he said, "if you will bow down and worship Me.*

—Matthew 4:8-9

90

The third temptation was at the level of defiance toward the person of God. This temptation involved the purpose of His coming into the world. Jesus came to redeem men, not to rule them. Satan's way, still followed by many, required no suffering and death, but Jesus chose God's way, the way of the cross. Jesus came here to be given as the perfect sacrifice for the sins of the the world—to die on the cross. . Now He is being presented with an alternative to God's "perfect" plan by none other than Satan himself. Satan actually offered the world back, without a shot being fired. Jesus only had to do one thing: fall down and worship Satan. Had Jesus given in to this temptation, we would have had another Garden of Eden situation—another fall like that of the first Adam.

★

They see me preaching on television but they do not understand the weight of praying for ten thousand people.

★

In summary, Christ had to walk away from bread, which His flesh was craving. He turned His back on the pride found in testing God when the devil dared Him to fall and be caught by a thousand angels. He chose God's plan over Satan's for reclaiming the kingdoms of the world instead of giving worship to the devil. Look into your life and find out those emotional disciplines you ought to have and try to ensure they are similar to what Jesus had.

Just as Christ had the emotional discipline to walk away from temptation, I am obligated to have the same emotional discipline when people are overwhelmed and see me as a celebrity but fail to see the service. They see me preaching on television but they do not understand the weight of praying for ten thousand people. I have to have an emotional discipline not to be caught up in the fanfare and forget to stabilize in the faith.

You really don't know your true strength until you have gone through a test and trial. I confess this was no bonus round when dealing with pressure. I was unable to sleep at night, lost ten pounds, had an irregular heartbeat, and my diet was inconsistent. In the area of my spiritual life, it was hard to discern the difference between praying and crying.

Though a natural extrovert, I saw myself slipping into the role of an introvert. I didn't want to entertain friends, answer the phone, or even go out. In this season I felt like all the world was talking about me and knew about my moral failure.

It is only through pressure you find your power. Anyone interested in developing their muscles, toning their body, or getting into shape understands the results are not realized without the consistent strain of pressure. To develop into the man God wanted me to be, He knew casual aerobic exercise would not suffice. I needed a great deal of pressure for the true muscle definition of my character, accountability, and integrity to develop. If you are going to go through this process, brace yourself for pressure.

SECTION II

Chapter 8

STRATEGY FOR WAR

—★—

He said: Listen, King Jehoshaphat and all who live in Judah and Jerusalem! This is what the Lord says to you: "Do not be afraid or discouraged because of this vast army. For the battle is not yours but God's."

—2 Chronicles 20:15

Not long ago I went for a crusade in Uganda, East Africa, along with my camera crew. I arrived there on Thursday night and found the people waiting and excited. In the meeting, we had delegates from Kenya, Tanzania, Ethiopia, Somalia, Sudan, Rwanda, Congo, Burundi, Nigeria, Malawi, and South Africa. Virtually all corners of Africa were represented in that meeting dubbed R.I.O.T. (Righteous Invasion of Truth) '06. My host, Pastor Robert Kayanja of The Miracle Center Cathedral gave me an awesome invite where I met the President and the entire first family of Uganda. The ten thousand five hundred seat cathedral was filled with young men and women energetically praising, fervently praying, and totally fired up for Jesus. On Friday evening I was welcomed onto the stage to deliver my second sermon. I preached that *"Time is of the Essence,"* and after the sermon I began to flow in the miraculous, with signs and wonders following. While people were being delivered, something strange happened. I heard a cry from the back of the sanctuary. Immediately I moved from the pulpit and went toward the back with my armor bearers and support staff to investigate where this cry was coming from, because I knew it was not the sound of the sacred. It was another kind of shout. When I reached the scene, I found a young woman in her mid-twenties crying. I could see her spirit was troubled and so I began to pray for her. She began to push chairs and fight for her life saying, "Please don't kill me." For all my years of preaching and praying I had never encountered anything on this level face-to-face. My armor bearer who is six-feet-three inches and two hundred thirty pounds couldn't intervene on my behalf. He simply stood behind me, because even with all of his training, he had no training to deal with spiritual warfare on this level.

There comes a time in life where you meet face-to-face with something you have never been trained or equipped for and have never experienced.

96

There comes a time in life where you meet face-to-face with something you have never been trained or equipped for and have never experienced. I began praying and asking God to equip me with skills, tools, and insight that I had never asked for or needed. I couldn't pray in a regular format like one does over their meal in a restaurant. I couldn't just recite scriptures like I did in Sunday school class. I couldn't start looking for a bowl of water or for anointing oil. I needed a new skill set for a new challenge and a new level. When you are in the midst of warfare, you must always remember that strategic adaptation is very important. When David went to fight Goliath, Saul wanted to put clothes on him that were not his size. David, however, had the sense and wisdom to know that he couldn't fight in someone else's regalia. He had to disrobe himself and go with what he knew to use. He learned how to use a sling-shot from fighting wild animals. He had never learned how to use a sling-shot on a giant, but he had to adjust. Everything you've experienced in your past has trained you in some way for the present fight. You just have to learn how to strategize.

For all the reading and premarital counseling I underwent prior to marriage, I never had a strategy for a successful marriage. Prior to being married, I was never in a successful monogamous relationship. Marriage was my first attempt.

Like millions of others, I assumed that after you get married, your previous struggles resolve themselves. It is not by accident those who operate recovery centers teach their patients/clients to say for the rest of their lives they are still in recovery, even when the program is over. The strongest alcoholic is not found in a bar. The most passionate drug addict does not spend free time in a crack house. But what do you do when your vice is always around you? Since my days in college, it became evident my weakness would be women. To this day I can boast I have never had a drink, not even champagne. I have never put drugs in my body unless they were prescribed by a doctor. Unfortunately, the one thing I was addicted to, there was no group support for help.

Five years into my marriage, while my former wife was taking care of our newborn twins, I relapsed into my weakness by engaging in an extramarital affair. I kept telling myself I would end it. I knew it was wrong. I feared being exposed; however, I continued to break my marital covenant for my own pleasure. At the point you say you can stop but do not, you have a problem. When you agonize over your dysfunction and realize it must end, recognize too, that it will not happen through osmosis. You need a strategy.

The word *strategy* comes from the ancient Greek word *strategos*, meaning literally the leader of the army. Ulysses S. Grant, a great general during the Civil War and America's eighteenth president said, "You don't need thirty-six strategies. The Art of War is simple enough. Find out where your enemy is. Get at him as soon as you can. Strike at him as hard as you can and as often as you can and keep moving on!"

Not long ago, while attending a men's only conference with Bishop T.D. Jakes in Texas, one of our ministerial mentors shared that on the back door of every hotel room there is a layout chart. In case of emergency it showed where the nearest exit was, where the elevator was, and there was a red dot that said, "This is where you are!" It doesn't matter where the emergency exit is if you don't know where you are. So many of us have launched an attack prematurely because we are looking for the enemy, but we aren't true to ourselves. When you realize where you are in the middle of the battle then you are better equipped to take on the strategy for warfare. The Bible gives us an account, in 2 Chronicles 20:15–20, of six strategies for war.

The first strategy is verse 15, *"Do not be afraid."* In the Bible there are sixty-two times that express the words, *"Do not be afraid."* It is significant because there is a fear in every second of every minute. The bible says, *Fear not* three hundred sixty-five times. In other words, for every day of the year there is a word of God for you not to be afraid. If you are afraid in the middle of the battle, you are going to lose because you are not success motivated. Remember that greater is He that is in you than he that is in the world and conquer your fear. (1 John 4:4) Fear will never change your circumstances; fear will never conquer your enemy. Fear tolerated is faith contaminated. You can't be fearful and faithful at the same time; one gives way to the other. The scripture clearly states in II Timothy 1:7, *"For God has not give us a spirit of fear, but of power, and of love, and of a sound mind."(nkjv)* We are to affirm ourselves and each other:, *"The Lord is the strength of my life; of whom shall I be afraid?"* (Psalm 27:1 nkjv)

While you face the battle of your life, ask yourself the most critical question, "Am I more fearful, or am I more faithful?"

While you face the battle of your life, ask yourself the most critical question, "Am I more fearful, or am I more faithful?" And by the way, you don't need to have a whole lot of faith. With faith the size of a mustard seed you can tell any mountain to get out of your way. (Matthew 17:20)

There is an old Japanese story of the Tea Master and the Ruffian that makes this point. The Lord of Tosa Province in Japan, Lord Yamanouchi, was going to Edo (now Tokyo) on an official trip and insisted that his tea master accompany him. The tea master was reluctant. He wasn't a sophisticated city person and not a samurai. He was afraid of Edo and the dangers he might face, but he was unable to refuse his master's request. His master, however, in a conscious attempt to bolster the tea master's confidence, attired him in Samurai clothing with the customary two swords. The Lord Yamanouchi thought that among the other samurai on the trip, the tea master would become invisible.

One day after arriving in Edo the tea master decided to take a walk. The very danger he feared, most then confronted him. A ronin, a masterless samurai, approached him, insisting it would be an honor to try out his skills in swordsmanship against a samurai of the Tosa province. In reality all the ronin really wanted was the tea master's money, which he could get if he killed him.

The shock of this confrontation, at first, immobilized the tea master so much that he couldn't even speak. Finally gaining a little composure, the tea master explained he was not really a samurai and didn't want a confrontation, but the ronin pressed harder. He demanded a test of skills. He said it

100

would be an insult to the province of Tosa if its honor wasn't defended.

The tea master didn't know what to do at this point. After thinking it over for a while he saw no way out of the situation. He became resigned to dying, but then he remembered he had earlier passed a school of swordsmanship. The tea master said to the ronin, "If you insist, we will test our skills, but first I must finish an errand for my master and will return later when the errand is completed." The ronin, now pumped up with confidence, readily agreed. The tea master made his way back to the school of swordsmanship. Luckily, the master was in and would see him. The tea master explained his situation and asked the sword master how he might behave correctly, to die like a samurai, so as to uphold his province's honor. The sword master was surprised. He answered that most come to learn how to hold and use a sword, whereas he had come instead to learn how to die. "Serve me a cup of tea," said the sword master, "while I will think the situation over."

The tea master cleared his mind. He knew this might be the last cup of tea he might ever serve. He began his preparation, a practice ritual performed as if nothing else existed, each movement being a total concentration on the moment, on the action. Impressed with this performance, the sword master said, "That's it."

"Tomorrow," said the sword master, "when you face the ronin, use this same state of mind. Think of serving tea to a guest. Apologize for the delay. And when you take off your outer garment, fold it, and place your fan upon it with the same calm assurances and grace that you use in preparation of tea. Continue this focus as you rise and put on your headband. Draw your sword slowly, raise it above your head, and hold it there, like this," he said, "and close your eyes. When you hear a yell, strike down. It will probably end in mutual slaying."

After thanking the sword teacher the tea master returned to meet the ronin, resigned to his fate. Following his instructor's advice, the tea master apologized for the delay and began to prepare himself ceremoniously—carefully taking off his outer garment, folding it, and then placing his fan on top. The ronin was startled. This fearful figure, who once said he was but a lowly tea master, had changed. Now before him was total concentration, poise, and confidence— someone fearless and controlled. The tea master finally faced his foe and raised his sword as he had been shown. He closed eyes awaiting the shout that would seal his fate, but nothing happened. Seconds later when he finally opened his eyes, there was no ronin to be seen, but only a small figure in the distance quickly receding away.

Within the church there are many people who dress like Christians and so the devil expect them to know who declare themselves to be Christian, carried on outside the church as they do inside those wall..the devil expects you to know how to fight. If the same way people professed Christianity while in the church was the same way they carried themselves in the face of attack, then the devil would see them praising God everywhere they go, he would back off and think he messed with the wrong person.

Tomorrow march down against them. They will be climbing up by the Pass of Ziz, and you will find them at the end of the gorge in the Desert of Jeruel.

—2 Chronicles 20:16

Verse 16 presents to us the second strategy, which is, "Know where your enemy resides." The enemy resides in the path of *Ziz*, which translates to mean flower or delicate. Your enemy looks good but they've got nothing good for you. Looks like they are successful but it means nothing to you. Don't be intimidated by people's surface value. Some people who appear to have everything, if followed behind closed doors, are on the verge of catastrophe emotionally, physically, financially or relationally. They are going through the desert of Jeruel, which means fear. They are delicate and afraid. This is precisely why the enemy is ferociously attacking you; because, in all reality, he is threatened by you. Your enemies are insecure. If they knew their identity and purpose, they wouldn't be spending so much energy trying to deflate you. They've been living in a desert of fear. The reason why they attacked was because in their area things were not growing. They weren't experiencing any progress in their lives. Anybody who spends their time attacking you– if you take notice– they are doing nothing with their lives. If you are focused on your vision, you will have no time to tear other people down.

Do not be afraid or discouraged because of this vast army. For the battle is not yours, but God's.

—2 Chronicles 20:15b

103

Strategy number three, is in verse 15: "What you are fighting against is bigger than you. Your opponent has more soldiers and weapons than you do but take delight in knowing that the battle is not yours but the Lord's." God will take care of your bills and help you raise your children. For anything that has been assigned to kill you, simply let go and let God. Like one philosopher put it, "Kill with a borrowed sword." When you come through the attack, your hands will be clean. If you hold your peace and let the Lord fight your battles, if you focus on God, God will handle everything just fine.

You will not have to fight this battle. Take up your positions; stand firm, and see the deliverance the Lord will give you, O Judah and Jerusalem. Do not be afraid; do not be discouraged. Go out to face them tomorrow, and the Lord will be with you.

—2 Chronicles 20:17

There's yet another strategy—strategy number four—in verse 17: position yourself. Set yourself in your position and get ready to see what God will do. You don't have to be somebody else. Whatever position you are in, play your role. Once you find your role, stay in your lane and do what you do best.

Strategy number five: Keep your position. Stand still and see the salvation of the Lord. Ephesians 6 reminds us that after we've done all we can: stand. When I was young we used to play the game, *Red Light, Green Light*. When someone hollered you had to stop and when they said green light you were allowed to keep moving until you heard red light. God is giving you a green light to praise Him. When the red light comes on, you stand still to see God move. Praise God like nothing will ever stop you.

The sixth strategy gets a little uncomfortable for many of us because it calls for waiting. But still, "Wait until tomorrow." The war you are fighting or engaged in will be settled tomorrow. Whatever you have been trying to figure out, God promised you victory tomorrow. It will be handled, settled, and won in your favor. That is why you shouldn't wait until the battle is over, but praise God right in the midst of it.

★

The average soldier does not make a loud noise until he has victory. When you worship God, do not do it like you are uncertain.

★

Jehoshaphat bowed with his face to the ground, and all the people of Judah and Jerusalem fell down in worship before the Lord. Then some Levites from the Kohathites and Korahites stood up and praised the Lord, the God of Israel, with very loud voice.

—2 Chronicles 20:18–19

The average soldier does not make a loud noise until he has victory. When you worship God, do *not* do it like you are uncertain. Rather, do it like you know you have the victory. Don't praise God like you are defeated. God didn't need everybody to do it, but needed some people from Judah. Now, the people of Judah didn't know how to fight, but they knew how to worship God for victory until it manifested.

Early in the morning they left for the Desert of Tekoa...

—2 Chronicles 20:20

In verse 20 they were in the realm of Tekoa, which translates as confirmation. Know for a fact that this battle will be over sooner than you may think. By the time it's over, God will have confirmed to you what the call on your life is.

After consulting the people, Jehoshaphat appointed men to sing to the Lord and to praise Him for the splendor of His holiness as they went out at the head of the army, saying: "Give thanks to the Lord, for His love endures forever." As they began to sing and praise, the Lord set ambushes against the men of Ammon and Moab and Mount Seir who were invading Judah, and they were defeated.

—2 Chronicles 20:21–22

Everybody in the camp became successful because of the presence of worshipers. You too can worship your way to the victory.

Chapter 9

IMPLEMENTING THE BATTLE PLAN

★

I will extol the Lord at all times; His praise will always be on my lips.

—Psalm 34:1

As an undergraduate in college I majored in political science and international affairs. It was my intent at the time to pursue a career in international law. In class, one of the tasks assigned to us was to examine universal principles from varying cultural perspectives. We looked at marriage, hunger, education, crime, and punishment of crime all from the perspective of different cultures. While thinking about the chapters of this book, I was reminded of a warfare theories analysis I once read in class.

The philosophy of war, the explanation of how to fight and win, is dominated by two theories. They are as ancient as the history of mankind. One philosophy is European. The other is Asian.

European theory rests on developing an industrial base to produce and sustain an overwhelming militaristic force. You win by being brutally overpowering.

Asian military theory is built around the notion of deception. Armies are lightly armed and nimble. Lightning-quick strikes are used to deceive the enemy, expose a weakness, and exploit that weakness with precision.

The traditional European approach provides a detailed description of what ought to happen from the moment war is proclaimed until the peace treaty is signed. This is the classic western war of attrition. Armies win because they bring more troops to the fight than the enemy can handle. The industrial base produces more arms, planes, tanks than the opposition is capable of producing, and they do it faster than the weapons can be destroyed. The European approach applies solid plans, focused on concrete goals, which produces substantial, measurable results.

The Asian philosophy is different. Told in tidbits, hidden in proverbs that are sometimes obscure and contemplative in nature, it follows symmetry much like Solomon's proverbs. According to this approach, deception is the key element of war. The aim of military action is not to wipe out the entire army but to remove the opposing leadership. In eradicating the leadership you take control of the mind of the army.

Force is used sparingly and only as a last resort. An ideal victory is won without the loss of life.

One approach comes from destruction; the other from deception. One is cold and calculating; the other intellectual and acerbic. One appeals to the fist; the other to the mind.

In spiritual warfare, the enemy attempts to combine these two approaches in his attacks against the body of Christ. Satan wants to deceive us about who we are by getting us to doubt that we are joint heirs with Jesus Christ. The enemy has mastered European ideology, so he attacks your body to cause you to lose your objectivity. He wants you to forget that even when you are under attack, there is still a promise over your life. His aim is to get you focused on the attack, on the pain, and on the enemy, so you'll forget that the Lord said in Psalm 23:6, *"Surely goodness and love will follow me all the days of my life."*

★

Satan wants to deceive us about who we are by getting us to doubt that we are joint heirs with Jesus Christ.

★

Our newspapers often are filled with stories of stars and other socialites who find themselves in conflict with the law. Their stardom seems to convince them that they are above the law. They are deceived. That deception puts them in a position from which they could lose everything they've worked hard to gain. Deception, leading to total destruction. Martha Stewart, Paris Hilton, Lil' Kim, T.I., and Michael Vick are examples of stars who have found themselves in jail after falling victim to this deception. Either they believed the law didn't apply to them, or that they'd never get caught. This deception is part of a two-pronged attack to destroy their career and affect their destiny.

The paragon of deception and destruction is Mike Tyson. A multi-millionaire with the world at his fingertips, he was one of the youngest heavyweight champions of the world. Yet he found himself forced to fight for his life. He was put in that position because he thought the rules didn't apply to him. That approach landed him in prison.

———————★———————

It's not just the rich and famous who fall into that trap. I once thought I was above the law too.

———————★———————

It's not just the rich and famous who fall into that trap. I once thought I was above the law too.

At twenty-two years of age, I was chosen to be the NAACP's National Youth and College Director. More than sixty thousand young people were under my leadership. In spite of my earlier understanding that I was called to the ministry, I took that job thinking I would never be a pastor. Instead, I wanted to work as a civil rights activist full-time. I thought if I did that, I wouldn't be accountable to anybody.

110

The NAACP had more than five hundred college chapters and one thousand two hundred youth chapters nationwide. My work took me to a different city and college every week. With all the accolades and applause, I began to believe I was above the law. Not the constitutional law. I wasn't out there breaking federal and state laws. The law I ignored was God's covenant law. As a consequence, I gave myself over to the flesh. I began to believe that because of my popularity, oratorical skills, and youthful influence, the law of God wouldn't catch up with me.

Through my position with the NAACP, I appeared on CNN and other television news channels. Articles about me appeared in *USA Today, Jet* magazine, and *US News & World Report*. I was flying pretty high.

Then I got the shock of my life. My girlfriend called and said those three words a young man in my position does not want to hear: "I am pregnant."

To say I was broken and terrified wouldn't be adequate. The walls seemed to close in on me. In my spirit I repeated those words of Jesus.

"My God, why have you forsaken me?"

God was saying similar words to me.

"My son, why have you forsaken Me?"

Over and over, I pleaded with the Lord to take this trial away from me. It was going to affect my life, my career, and my family. In response, God said and did nothing.

My mother, a devoted woman of intercession, began to pray. She told me that this was not going to happen to me. She insisted that my girlfriend was not telling the truth and that it was not my child.

"Take a blood test," she said.

My mother, I believe, taps into the veil of God. She had interceded in many situations before and had never been wrong—until the day the results of the blood test arrived at my home. There was no denying the fact that I was the child's father.

My position, popularity, and influence deceived me into thinking this couldn't happen to me. I was destroyed on the inside. For a long time, I thought God had done this to me. It never occurred to me that I had actually done this to God.

When you get to a place where you feel like you are above the law, be prepared. The walls of your life are about to come crashing down. You might think, as I did, that you aren't accountable or responsible for your decisions. Nothing could be further from the truth. Your responsibility is firmly fixed. You can deny it. You can ignore it, but you can't avoid it. One way or the other, accountability for your decisions and conduct will come back to you.

Thankfully, I didn't destroy myself. I wallowed in self-pity a little, but not long enough to do any lasting damage. In the end, I understood that I was responsible for the consequences of my own decisions. Even now, that's a responsibility I do my best to fulfill.

This is how the enemy attacks those in the Kingdom of God. He comes with deception and destruction. His aim is to wipe you out. He wants to annihilate the army of God. He wants to obliterate us. He begins with deception, but he comes with a full-scale attack, bringing a force he wants you to think has overwhelming power. But don't believe him. God is still on your side, even when you fall for the enemy's lies. Turn to God in repentance, and He will turn to you in grace.

When you turn away from deception and destruction, you turn toward grace and mercy. You also turn toward responsibility and accountability. I couldn't blame the mother of my child for what happened. I was as much involved in the pregnancy as she was. I couldn't throw the blame on my parents either. They did their best to teach me how to act. In the end, I had to hold myself accountable. I understood that the enemy wanted to destroy me, but I knew one more thing. The things with which the enemy attacked for my destruction were the tools God would use to develop His character in me. All I had to do was yield to the discipline and discipleship of God. That's grace. God took what Satan meant for evil and turned it to His use for good—that was grace and mercy.

★

When you turn away from deception and destruction, you turn toward grace and mercy. You also turn toward responsibility and accountability.

★

113

In chapters 18 and 19 of Luke, God gives us the strategy for winning the war completely and do it without ever shedding one drop of *our* blood.

Look at the life of Jesus. He understood deception, He also understood His purpose. He knew who He was in the Kingdom of God; that He was seated at the right hand of the Father. When he walked into Jerusalem, He didn't ask for a stretch limousine, heavy-duty security, or white horses to usher Him into the city. He simply asked for the cheapest animal one can find—"Get me a colt and let me ride on it."

I'm sure back then people with limited understanding thought like they do today: "What you're riding on or in is a reflection of the power you possess. They think you only have the anointing if you are riding in a Mercedes, Lincoln, or Lexus. Jesus rode on a colt enabling those who loved and followed Him to shift their focus from His mode of transportation to the One who drove His passion.

You are the Lord's greatest undercover agent. You have deceived the enemy. Satan sees that you don't have a lot of necessities and thinks you'll turn from God. Yet your obedience to God is not contingent on the house you live in, the car you drive, or the clothes that are on your back. Those things don't make me who I am. They don't define your identity, either. Who we are is determined by who God, for we are His workmanship. Don't get me wrong and live in a nice house; but if those things could never be, I would wake up each morning confident that my integrity was intact and my heart belongs to God.

The problem with many people is that they have set themselves up for deception. They gauge their salvation by the fancy clothes, expensive cars, and whether they have a three-piece suit to wear. God would rather have you come into His presence wearing shorts and a T-shirt, glorifying Him for the great things He has done, than to have you driving a in a new car or wearing expensive clothes.

When Jesus arrived in Jerusalem, people were shouting, "Hosanna! Blessed is the Son of David!" While they sang and shouted, Jesus refused to get caught up in the moment. He knew how to be at ease around His enemies. When you know your purpose, you can't be intimidated by people. Whether they want to see you dead or are filled with envy and jealousy over your life. I'd doesn't matter.

When Jesus rode into Jerusalem, people climbed trees. They tore off palm branches and waved them in the air. They threw their clothes in the street for Him to ride across. All the while, Jesus knew that the following week, at about that same time of day, He was going to be crucified. The people who wanted to make Him king when He entered the city soon would be shouting for His death. Jesus didn't try to stop them. He accepted their praise, knowing they were going to turn on Him in just a few days. Jesus rode through Jerusalem at ease in the presence of His enemies and unmoved by their flattery. I'm sure he said to Himself, *Whatever happens to Me today will not affect My destiny tomorrow.*

Whatever it is you face at this time in your life, rest assured that the plans of the Lord for you will not be thwarted. Remind yourself, "The Lord's plans for me are for my good, and not my destruction. All that He allows will benefit my future and give me hope." (Jeremiah 29:11)

Jesus knew He was being celebrated that day, but was going to be scandalized in the days to come. He knew the people He'd helped would be the same ones who would hurt Him. He knew when He was on trial before Jewish and Roman authorities, the people He'd come to save would not be there to testifying His behalf. He was prepared for this in advance. This is what it means to have strategy.

One day God will bring you to a place where you no longer care what other people say about you. You'll know who you are in Christ.

When Jesus went to trial, no one showed up as a character witness. He didn't even defend Himself. Whatever the accusers said didn't move Him because He knew who He was. One day God will bring you to a place where you no longer care what other people say about you. You'll know who you are in Christ.

Job said, *"Though He slay me, yet will I hope in Him."* (Job 13:15) Then David said, *I will extol the Lord at all times; His praise will always be on my lips."* (Psalm 34:1)

Praise Him when your circumstances seem to overwhelm you. Praise Him when He vanquishes every enemy. Above all, praise Him because He is Lord of the universe, God of all time, and God of the promises over your life.

Chapter 10

A MIND TO SURVIVE

★

The mind of sinful man is death, but the mind controlled by the Spirit is life and peace.

—Romans 8:6

All of my life I have been afraid of needles. Even now, as a grown man, when I need an injection someone has to talk me through it. I do *not* like needles.

A few years ago, I went to the dentist for a root canal. As I sat in the dentist's chair, he reached out to me with a lollipop in his hand. His other hand was behind his back. He knows I don't like needles.

I said, "Is that a needle you've got back there?"

"Yes, Jamal, it's a needle."

"I don't want to take that needle. Is there anything else you can use to rub on my gums or something?"

He shook his head. "You have to get it done this way for now."

Knowing that I was quickly running out of options, I thought I might at least postpone my fate. "Give me a minute to compose myself. What's in that needle anyway?"

"Novocain."

For a moment I thought I'd found an escape.

"I can't take Novocain," I said. "Isn't that cocaine? I'm a minister of the Gospel. There could be something addictive to it."

The dentist informed me there was only a small amount of Novocain and reassured me it would only numb the pain. He had to drill deep into my tooth to fix it.

"Drill?" I exclaimed. "You have to drill? That's going to hurt."

"That's the beauty of Novocain. It numbs the pain. After that, it's just an operation of the mind."

"What do you mean?"

"After you take the Novocain, you'll feel the pressure of me working on that tooth, but you won't feel the pain."

"You sure about that?"

He nodded.

"Tell your mind not to confuse the pressure for pain."

That sentence struck me. Tell my mind that what I was experiencing was not pain, just pressure.

What a lesson. And what a way to learn it!

Sometimes, when you're faced with a tough battle, you come to a place in your mind where you don't want the quick "Novocain" or word that would ease the pain involved in the issues you face. Once you have accepted God's purpose for your life and faced the reality of that situation, you realize the pain you feared really wasn't pain at all. The real pain was the area you wanted to ignore. That unaddressed area worked as pressure that pushed you in the wrong direction. Pressure that was trying to get you to avoid dealing with an issue God wanted you to face. Pressure that would have driven you away from the cure.

To stick with the dentist's office theme, the pressure—pressure my mind perceived as pain—told me the root canal was painful, even though the Novocain had numbed my mouth to the point that I could barely talk. That perception of pain made me want to bolt out of that dentist's chair and run. I didn't care about the decay in my tooth. I just wanted to avoid the treatment. That pressure tried to force me in a particular direction, one that would take me away from the solution to my aching tooth. It's the same in spiritual warfare.

The emotional pressure you sense, often from people you've known for a long time, tries to push you in a particular direction. If you take a moment and think about what's really happening you'll see the pressure you feel, which your mind might interpret as pain, is trying to divert you away from a solution to your situation, from facing an issue you've avoided for a long time, or from an inner struggle you don't want to address. That pressure makes you want to run and hide. Hide in drugs, a spending spree, or an eating binge. You might just want to bury your head in the sand and ignore the problem and the treatment one more time. You've got to fight against the pressure.

Pressure like that comes from an area in your mind that has not yet been renewed; from thinking that is not yet in conformity with the mind of Christ. Satan plays on those areas of your mind and uses them for his purposes. He knows that if you ever address those issues, or if you press on through your circumstances, you are going to move up to the next level. God's gift to you is going to find a greater manifestation than you've ever known, and you are going to take a big step toward your destiny. Satan doesn't want that to happen.

He mounts up some pressure on you, points out how painful and difficult heading in the direction of your destiny will be then pushes you toward something easy—or at least requiring less effort than climbing the mountain to your summit where the view is glorious. This kind of attack doesn't happen in a vacuum. The pressure isn't theoretical. It's real. The pressure comes from your spouse, your former spouse, your in-laws—past and present—your boss, your brother, your best friend, or the person sitting beside you in church.

Many times an attack like this centers on an area of your mind where your thought processes have not been renewed. These are areas around which Satan has built spiritual strongholds.

Paul tells us, *"The mind of sinful man is death, but the mind controlled by the Spirit is life and peace; the sinful mind is hostile to God. It does not submit to God's law, nor can it do so. Those controlled by the sinful nature cannot please God."* (Romans 8:6-8)

Even after you commit your life to Christ, some areas of your mind are still trapped in the old way of thinking. There are people in church whose minds have been held captive for decades and they don't even know it.

> ★
>
> *Even after you commit your life to Christ, some areas of your mind are still trapped in the old way of thinking.*
>
> ★

Think about this: The preacher gets up to preach a sermon from Luke 12:22 where Jesus says, *"Therefore I tell you, do not worry about your life, what you will eat; or about your body, what you will wear."* (Luke 12:22) He lays out the text of that passage and gets everything ready for a really great message. Then the next thing you know, Satan's telling you, "Now, Jesus didn't really mean for you not to worry about tomorrow. We all have to plan and save."

Or a sermon based on Luke 18:18-22 where Jesus tells the rich young ruler, *"Sell all you own, give it to the poor, and come and follow me."* *(paraphrased)* We've all heard sermons on that text that start out well but before the preacher gets halfway through he qualifies his remarks with a statement like, *"Now, Jesus didn't mean for you to really sell everything you own."*

Statements like these reveal areas of unbelief. These are examples of beliefs that are inconsistent with Scripture—inconsistent with Jesus' own words. Each of those statements is really saying, *"God can't take care of you. You have to take care of yourself."* They are in direct opposition to the point Jesus made in those texts. Jesus was saying, *"Trust God with everything. Lay it all on the line. God really will take care of you."* Saying the opposite is saying God can't or won't do that. That's unbelief.

Now, Satan takes these areas of unbelief and builds around them a stronghold. Using the wrong understanding of these two passages of Scripture, as an example, Satan would build a financial stronghold grounded in this unbelief. It might manifest as one hording unto himself. More than likely, it's going to appear in the form of "veto" power. For instance, your bank account may hold "veto" power over whatever you hear God telling you to do. Let's say you know God directed you, saying, "Take that person to lunch," and then you check your bank statement or wallet to determine whether you have the money to buy them lunch. If you have enough money to cover everything, you'll gladly do as the Lord instructs, however, if you aren't sure you can stretch your money until the next payday, you won't. This is giving your bank account "veto" power over the holy Spirit. It comes from a financial stronghold that developed through unbelief. The truth is that you really don't believe what Jesus said. You don't believe God can or will meet your financial needs.

When you allow your perceived lack veto the will of God in your life, you rob God of the opportunity to work through you, and you rob others of a blessing God intended for them. That person the Holy Spirit wanted you to take to lunch might be a person in desperate need; whether it be a friend, an attentive ear, your experience in certain matter, or maybe their need is more simple, like a meal.

Strongholds formed through unbelief in your mind. Those strongholds limit the ability of God to work in your life. Jesus experienced this in His own hometown. He'd been out doing mighty acts of ministry, healing people and casting out demons. After a while, He returned to His hometown. Those miracles, signs, and wonders He'd done elsewhere suddenly became difficult to accomplish. Matthew 14:53–58 says it was because of their unbelief.

To combat these strongholds, Jesus puts you in places that shed light on your disbelief. unbelief to light. He wants to give you His mind (1 Corinthians 2:16). In order to do that, for your mind to become the mind of Christ, your mind must be renewed. Your thought processes must be transformed. This method of transformation is much like the cleansing Paul mentions in relation to the entire church where he says in Ephesians 5:26 God is *cleansing her by the washing with water through the word.*

Tearing down those strongholds requires you to go deeper into Scripture and to allow it to get deeper into you. Let Scripture speak for itself. And let the Holy Spirit show you the meaning, separate and apart from your own experience.

★

When the enemy occupies territory in your mind, he uses that as a base from which to unleash an unbridled attack on your psyche, self-esteem, and conscience.

★

When you sense this struggle, this tension from the pressure and perceived pain associated with a problem or issue, ask the Holy Spirit to take charge. Ask Him to show you the area of your mind that has not yet been renewed. Ask Him to show you the root of unbelief that has caused you to perceive this pressure as pain. Ask Him to show you the lie you've been holding onto. Ask Him to show you why you want to run and hide. He will show you and He will cleanse your mind and renew your thinking to bring it in line with the mind of Christ. This is a huge key to reaching the full manifestation of your gift and in reaching your destiny.

Facing those strongholds in your life can be scary at first. Like that needle in the dentist's hand, it looks painful. If you don't allow the Holy Spirit to tear down those strongholds, you will only be subjected to progressively worse attacks, and you will be robbed of your destiny. When the enemy occupies territory in your mind, he uses that as a base from which to unleash an unbridled attack on your psyche, self-esteem, and conscience.

In order to break free of those strongholds, you have to know that comfort is not your friend. It is not your greatest need. Comfort is not essential to survival. Growth, renewal, regeneration, transformation: these are essential. Not the ease and comfort the pressure in your life pushes you toward. In your physical body, pain is an indication something is wrong. It's your body's way of telling you where the problem is located. You ignore it at great peril. That same thing occurs in your spiritual life.

Comfort—the easy way— is the way to hell. That's why Jesus said in Matthew 7:13–14, "*Enter through the narrow gate. For wide is the gate and broad is the road that leads to destruction, and many enter through it. But small is the gate and narrow the road that leads to life, and only a few find it.*" The wrong way looks easy from the beginning. It gets worse and worse the farther you go. The right way looks hard at the beginning, but once you break through that first part, it gets easier.

As soon as you feel pain, begin to shout and move toward the source of that pain. Lean into it. I know this sounds twisted but you have to thank God for the pain because that pain lets you know where the enemy is residing. We talked about this earlier. The enemy resides in fear. When you sense fear, you know that's where the enemy is located. It's the same thing with pain. When you sense emotional pain, that's where the enemy is located. He's coming from the source of that pain. An unfaithful partner? The enemy is in the midst of it. Stand up and praise God. Start praising God. People around you won't understand why you shout and celebrate. It's not because you're feeling good, but you know you are shouting yourself through the pain. Start shouting praises to God and ask Him to show you the stronghold from which that pain was launched. Ask Him to show you the unbelief around which that stronghold was built. When He shows you that unbelief, repent of it. Lay it down at His feet and leave it. Then ask Him to infuse into you the true belief.

> *Whatever pain you are going through, won't last forever. Jesus had to go through the cross to get to the crown.*

Pain is always temporary. Whatever pain you are going through, won't last forever. Jesus had to go through the cross to get to the crown. If you want to get to the resurrection, you have to endure the cross. The cure for your situation might be painful, but it won't last long. The blessing from the solution will last forever. Start planning for what you are going to do when the pain is over. That pain will not always be there.

Don't get frustrated because you have these issues in your life that have to be addressed. When you're at war, you have to learn to deal with pain, discomfort, and seasons of dryness and frustration. Frustration is an attempt by the enemy to destroy your self-worth. Everyone who ever tried to accomplish anything of value has had moments of frustration. There are situations where you have pushed two steps ahead but then someone or something pulls you back. This is where your triumph starts to show. The enemy thinks he has frustrated you in reaching God's purpose, but you can frustrate him by rising up to fight one more time. It doesn't matter how many times you have failed in your life, try again. Jesus put you on this road, and He will see you to the end. As it says in Hebrews 12:2, *"He is the author and perfecter of our faith."*

When Joseph had a dream that his brothers were going to be his servants, his brothers started to plot for his failure. They threw him into an abandoned well. They thought they could change his attitude by taking him captive and subjecting him to conditions in that pit. Joseph was a prisoner of war—the greater war being waged by spiritual forces in the heavens. But Joseph said, "I know the dream and the One who gave it to me. This is not what I saw. I am not going to feel depressed and I am not going to commit suicide. God showed me a vision and this is not what the Lord showed me." (Genesis 37)

Everyone who ever tried to accomplish anything of value has had moments of frustration.

Then Judah, one of Joseph's brothers, came up with the idea of selling him as a slave. They took him out of the pit

127

and sold him to the Ishmaelites. Joseph was then sold into Egypt, where he later ended up in Jail. Now that is what I call double trouble: a slave and a prisoner all in one. But even then, while in jail, he told his fellow prisoners that his captivity was only temporary. He told himself this too.

You have to tell yourself the same things. A bounced check is not the fullness of God's vision for your life. It's not a good thing to bounce checks, but it's not the end either. A small apartment is not the fullness of the vision. God has given you a gift. He will bring that gift to full and abundant expression in your life. So speak to those things which are not as though they already are.

God wants to enter those dark places. He wants to take all that stuff that Satan throws at you and use it to make a beautiful picture. There's nothing more beautiful than the picture of a life colored with forgiveness. The Holy Spirit can take every instance where you made a mistake, rebelled, chose your own way, and He can brush that into the texture of your life. Those things that Satan uses to try and make you feel defeated, God will use to point you toward your destiny. Often-times, God goes into the deepest, most hidden, darkest areas in your heart and life where sin has gotten a foothold, and does His work there. Those are the places of unbelief. Those dark places are the strongholds from which Satan launches his attacks. Let God show you.

Your first level of defeat is when you are defeated in your mind. If you don't think that any given thing can be accomplished then it will not be done. But if you set your mind to it and believe in your heart it is going to take place then no matter what happens on the outside, it has got to manifest. If we can just conquer the inadequacies of our thinking, if we can talk ourselves out of negative thoughts then we will overcome. Whenever you get thoughts, or encounter people who say it can't be done then you have to shake off those words up and say, "If God said to me that it was going to happen then there is nothing in the earth that will be able to stop it." Determine today to destroy the number one killer of your dreams, which is a scaled-down identity of who you are in Christ. Get it in your mind that you could have been defeated a long time ago if that was God's purpose for your life, but daily He preserves you so that He can coach you toward victory.

Your first level of defeat is when you are defeated in your mind. If you don't think that any given thing can be accomplished then it will not be done.

Take the medicine. Take the shot. Confront those strongholds head-on and allow God to renew your mind. Allow Him to give you the mind of a conqueror. Allow Him to give you the mind of Christ.

Chapter 11

DEFEATING THE PAST

★

"Brothers, I do not consider myself yet to have taken hold of it. But one thing I do: Forgetting what is behind and straining toward what is ahead, I press on toward the goal to win the prize for which God has called me heavenward in Christ."

—Philippians 3:13–14

On one occasion my father came to visit our church. At the time we were doing three services on Sunday, averaging an hour and a half each. My father questioned me saying, "Why are you not using more denominational liturgy that stabilizes the church? As a bishop there is a standard of tradition." In spite of all the growth and tremendous strides as I was endeavored to set a new paradigm for the millennium ministry, he held fast to the traditions of the past. Had I held to the past I am not sure if Empowerment Temple would have the hope of being a church in the future. Tradition is an appreciation, affection, and staunch protection of the past. Innovation is a feat of faith without a foundation—faith is the substance of things hoped for.

In light to my belief and experience, I recommend innovation instead of tradition. Traditionally, in our denomination, you don't start a church. You wait for a pastor to die, retire, or get involved in a scandal, then you inherit the church. In my scenario, I established my church and held my first service in a nightclub that had different ballrooms. One sat five hundred and the other two hundred fifty. I set up the five hundred room with the capacity for five hundred. My parents came in from Texas to visit a few weeks before I opened. Dad looked at the rooms and said, 'This room is too big. You are setting yourself up for failure. You ought to move to the smaller one." What it showed me, in essence, is he was fighting other people's past failures. It was a battle between failures of the past and faith of the future.

Recently I read a book by Robert Greene, *The 33 Strategies of War*. Green talks about Napoleon Bonaparte who rose to power in just ten years, from captain in the French revolutionary army to brigadier general. He became the first consul of France in 1801 and an emperor in 1804. Napoleon was a genius of war, however, not everyone was impressed by his strength and quick rise to power. There were Prussian generals who thought he had merely been lucky. His adversaries believe that Napoleon Bonaparte's victories were a fluke because he didn't stick with the regimented guidelines of how war ought to be fought. They believed if they ever got an opportunity to fight Napoleon on the battleground they would win, because they knew all the regiments and the disciplinary techniques of winning war. They had studied intently the victories of Frederick the Great, who calculated war as a mathematical enterprise. You have to be careful what you ask for because not long after, they received a six weeks' notice to get ready for the greatest war of their lives. They brought into their war room all of their top advisers and they plotted out strategies of how to win the war against Napoleon Bonaparte.

There was a critical problem because all of the advisors were aged seventy and over. They didn't realize the cost of warfare had shifted and changed considerably. They were then planning for a war in a style that was no longer on the battleground. It is very important to carefully select who you listen to and count on as an advisor. You can only afford to listen to people who are fighting a similar kind of war you are facing right now. If you were a parent twenty years ago, much of your advice would be antiquated for raising a teenagers in this day and age. You have to deal with the person who has been in the most recent battlefield because if one has been off of the war game for a long time, then they lose touch. The people you need to have around you are those with fresh wounds because the memories are pain is still vivid in their mind and flesh. Some people who haven't had a struggle in a long time become judgmental. You need people who have been where you have are and can coach you as you fight to overcome. This is why it's not good to have judgmental people in your life. They don't know that each day of your life you are engaged in battle to become better.

The Prussians found themselves on the battleground not knowing that the rules of engagement had changed. The adversaries came with chariots, wagons, and all of their artillery, but those who were enlisted to fight with Napoleon came with their arsenal on backpacks.

The enemy is about to mess up because he thinks you have to go to a certain place to get more strength, yet God had equipped and empower you against the enemy. The Prussians began to get into their automated formation. When the drum would sound, they would shifted their formation and prepared for warfare. Napoleon would not put all of his soldiers on a straight line but attacked from every angle. Every time the Prussians saw they were losing the battle they would change the formation thinking the change might to shift the battle.

Understand that the enemy can't figure you out, so he keeps changing his formation. Maybe the devil thought he would be able to break you when the relationship did not work out, but you got back up and continued to fight. The devil is presently changing formation because he cannot figure out how to break you. Probably everything you have gone through should have driven you to give up, but thank God you woke up this morning with a fighter in you still kicking and that you have refused to be broken.

The adversaries discounted too early the strategy and the style of Napoleon. They thought the soldiers were unruly and undisciplined because they didn't go in a line. They claimed

Napoleon was not uncooperative. As for Napoleon, his response was that everybody didn't have to be doing the same thing in order to get the same objective accomplished. In the camp there was a method behind the madness because everybody had a different strength. What one couldn't successfully accomplish, another could. The problem with fighting in the present is that many people have been handicapped by the past. They are still fighting the past. Habits can become debilitating and repetition will block creativity. Consider Jesus' healing ministry, for instance: Every time Jesus healed, He never healed the same way twice. Sometimes He would just speak to a condition and other times He would lay hands. In either case, healing was imparted. When God decides to bless you, He may not do so in the same fashion that He blessed somebody else.

Every time Jesus healed, He never healed the same way twice. Sometimes He would just speak to a condition and other times He would lay hands.

At Morehouse College there is a sort of creed taken from the poem, 'Be Strong' by Maltbie Davenport,

"We are not here to play, to dream, to drift;

We have hard work to do, and loads to lift;

Shun not the struggle – face it; 'tis God's gift..."

When God puts a burden on your back, understand that your process will never match another's process. You cannot shun your own process in preference of another's because God is taking you to a different place.

As you fight, the enemy thinks he knows you by judging you based on previous responses. You have to do something different. There is an old adage, "You have to do something you've never done to get something you've never had."

Napoleon Bonaparte said, "Anyone can plan a campaign, but few are capable of waging war, only few can handle the development of circumstances that are not in your favor." Some people will never win because they cannot handle losing. You will only win when you know how to lose and still have hope.

> ★
>
> *When you are involved in warfare, do not fight from your history, fight from your heart.*
>
> ★

Job in the Bible lost all he had, and his wife urged him to curse God and die but Job's response from the beginning was, "The Lord gaves and the Lord has taken away; May the name of the Lord be praised." (Job 1:21) The enemy gets frustrated when you lose but praise God like a winner. Not everybody can win the war at the same time. For some, when the odds are against them, they retreat and act defeated. In fact, many times there are people who win because others forfeit their position when they allowed discouragement and hardship to defeat them.

When you are involved in warfare, don't fight from your history, fight from your heart. Choose to forget everything you learned about warfare in the past and know this is a brand-new ball game. Experience and theory have limitations, but wisdom is limitless. Remember, experience is based on information from the past, theory is hypothetically based on something that has never happened. Due to its timely nature, wisdom is by far the most reliable. When you have wisdom, it doesn't matter how the enemy attacks. God gives you understanding and discernment to know what the best option for you is in any given situation.

At one time, I was introduced to a television show *Deal or No Deal* hosted by actor/comedian Howie Mandel on NBC. The game of odds and chance unfolds when a contestant is confronted with twenty-six sealed briefcases. Each briefcase contains cash in amounts ranging from a penny to one million dollars. Without knowing the dollar amount in any of the briefcases, the contestant chooses one. He is to keep the one he chose, until it's opening at the end of the game. The risk element comes into play when the contestant must begin eliminating the remaining twenty-five cases, which are opened and the amount of cash inside revealed. The pressure mounts as in each round, after a pre-determined number of cases are opened. The contestant is tempted by a mysterious entity known only as *The Bank* to accept an offer of cash in exchange for what may be contained in the contestant's chosen briefcase. This prompts Mandel to ask the all-important question: Deal or no deal? As each case is opened, the likelihood of the contestant having a valuable cash prize in his briefcase increases or decreases. If the larger cash prizes haven't been opened, his chances increase. It shows if fortune really favors the bold; the contestant knows as long as the larger cash prizes have not been opened, *The Bank's* deals will only get higher. And if the torn contestant unwittingly opens a case with a higher cash value, *The Bank's* offer could suddenly vaporize. The Bank makes offers in order for the contestant not to meet his big goal. The genius producer of the show must have read Proverbs 11:14. "Where there is no counsel, the people fall; but in the multitude of counselors there is safety." (nkjv) Do not settle for mediocrity or anything less than what God promised you. Go all the way and attain what God promised you. Tell the devil, "No deal. I will not settle for what you are offering because I have a better deal up ahead. "

As I watched the show, there were many peculiar dynamics. One contestant had friends who prodded, "No deal!" While the family cried, "Settle, you've made enough money already." The friends exhorted her, saying she had come too far to quit.

There are times when God will require you to bi-pass what your family says about you and what friends think. Be certain you are on the path God is blessing, regardless of the many voices around you. Determine not to compromise or stop until you have tasted all God has set in motion and promised you. Maybe you are in one of the most painful, potentially devastating battles of your life, and you do not understand why. The answer is simple: Satan, the enemy of your soul, does not want you to make it to the finish line. But take heart, this means he's frightened of what you'll do when you DO reach your destiny. It's time for you to intensify your side of the battle. You have made too much progress to give up.

It's interesting that in many cases your fight isn't coming from strangers. It's coming from people with whom you are well acquainted. Sadly, those closest to you usually can't see the changes God has made in you. They're stuck in your former ways of handling life, and you can't seem to convince them to see you differently. Many of them may be surprised when you do achieve all you said. But don't allow that to discourage you. God has destined you to win, and you will. Part of your fight right now is to break free from who you used to be. The devil and all his minions are determined to get you back to who you used to be, but you have to be determined never to go back. Head for your future because God wants to show the world you were delivered from your past. The enemy wants to hold you a prisoner to how you used to think, act, and live. If you surrender your life to God, whatever you did in the past ceases to be held against you. You can stop running from your past and face the future with boldness.

> *It's interesting that in many cases your fight isn't coming from strangers. It's coming from people with whom you are well acquainted.*

The war is not about your present, but about your potential. The enemy wants to abolish your potential by holding you hostage to your past. God loves you despite your worst, and He'll love you when you get to your best. A lot of people don't like you, based on rumors they have heard about you. God, however, loves you even though He has evidence against you. He still loves you because you will always remain valuable to Him.

> ★
>
> *As a young generation, we are not compromising the gospel message by what we are doing nor are we conforming to the world. Instead, we seek to meet our generation where they are.*
>
> ★

Not long ago I participated with about fifty church leaders on a Word Network forum entitled *Voices of the Black Church*. While discussing the topic of the New Age Era, I was asked by one of the seasoned fathers of the faith who came along in a generation not allowed to listen to secular music, "Aren't we bordering on accommodation rather than preaching transformation? The Bible admonishes us not to be conformed to this world."

In my response, I mentioned the city of Troy. One of the most famous cities in history, it was known throughout the world for being impenetrable. The Greeks wanted to seize the city because of the resources it contained. Somebody from another generation suggested, "Stop trying to climb the wall. Let's build a wooden horse."

They built the wooden horse in order to gain access to the city. Once the horse was constructed, well-armed men hid inside. The horse was left outside Troy's walls as a peace offering from the Greeks. The Trojans found the horse and pulled it inside the city. At midnight, the Greek soldiers vacated the horse, killed the guards, and opened the gates of the city. Where the previous generation threw rocks over the wall and was never able to penetrate the gates, a new generation used creative thinking and accomplished the goal they set.

As a young generation, we are not compromising the gospel message by what we are doing nor are we conforming to the world. Instead, we seek to meet our generation where they are. In a testimony, there must be a level of transparency. Regrettably the previous generations handed to us a certificate of the witness protection program. This certificate said, "Don't talk about what you have been through and what you are." However, our generation is filled with living testimonies of the perfecting process.

One of the glaring microcosms is the talk about rap music in religiosity. Just like the old school put women in another forum separate from men, it is the same derogatory forum that rap music would be. Those in hip-hop culture know that good music is not just hip hop but has taken R&B classic. Hence, we are not trying to reinvent the wheel; we are just adding rims on it with spinners.

Most front runners in the new generation of preachers are seminary trained and have been through ordination. We have not forsaken what we are, but we understand we are preaching to MTV, BET, and the X generation. Most of this group does not know a church hymn; however, if they can come to church with Jay-Z on their iPods and Beyoncé CDs in the car, by the time they leave the church, they will be able to say, "Just as I am without one plea."

Chapter 12

FIGHTING FOR CONTROL

★

When a man's ways are pleasing to the Lord, He makes even His enemies live at peace with him.

—Proverbs 16:7

It takes focus and perspective for you to not surrender your self-control when your temper starts to boil. While on the cross, Jesus had plenty of opportunities to curse those around Him. Instead, He blessed them.

From a human point of view, Jesus had good reason to be mad. He fed five thousand men, women, and children but was left dangling on the cross. He spent hours and hours teaching truths and concepts that had never even been thought in the entire history of the world. He healed and He restored. And now some of those He'd helped were the ones in the crowd jeering and calling for His death. Does this sound anything like the people you've helped?. You bailed them out, but now when you need help they are nowhere to be found. People see you in a mess and won't lift a finger to help. It makes you want to curse.

When Jesus faced that same situation, He didn't anything. He didn't utter a word. The last time anyone heard a word from Him was in court. The authorities listed all the charges they had against Him and the only thing He ever said was, "You say so." He didn't defend Himself. He didn't need to. He understood who He was. What they said about Him didn't change a thing.

> *From a human point of view, Jesus had good reason to be mad. He fed five thousand men, women, and children but was left dangling on the cross.*

Jesus didn't say anything when they made a crown of thorns and put it on His head. He didn't say anything when the blood began dripping in His eyes. He didn't say anything even when none of the disciples showed up to pay bail or argue as a character witnesses. He was hung between two thieves who listened to hear what He would say and all He said was, "Father, forgive them..."

That's self-control.

God gives you divine permission to be silent in the face of ignorance. Some people don't merit the sound of your voice.

You have authority over how you respond to the people who are attacking you. You don't have to respond at all.

Not only did Jesus exercise control over His response, He forgave those who put Him on that cross. Forgiving those who've wronged you isn't just a nice thing to do. It isn't a mere suggestion either. It's a command. Obedience to that command is crucial. They may not deserve your forgiveness. They may not want your forgiveness. But like many other things in the Christian life, you need to give it to them. The command to forgive those who have offended you isn't a command for their benefit. It's for your benefit.

When you harbor un-forgiveness and resentment, you tie yourself to the person who offended you.

When you harbor un-forgiveness and resentment, you tie yourself to the person who offended you. Psychologically and spiritually, you become bound to that person and to the pain and injury they inflicted. You think you're getting back at them by holding it against them. In reality, they are poisoning you. That poison will work its way through every aspect of your soul, tainting your mind, will, and emotions. If you don't break free of them, you will become just like that person. The very characteristics about them you hold in such disdain will become your own characteristics. God has given you the tool to break free from them. That tool is forgiveness, which is the way to freedom. Forgiveness cuts you free of them, forever. You aren't letting them off the hook. They're still accountable to God for whatever they did. You're letting yourself off the hook.

You have the authority to forgive. Forgiveness is a powerful weapon of spiritual warfare. Whatever happened to you during your childhood, while you were in college, or on the job. Say to everyone who hurt you, "I forgive you." And if you can't say it directly to them, go before your Father and declare, "Father, I forgive them."

★

You have the authority to forgive. Forgiveness is a powerful weapon of spiritual warfare.

★

Jesus forgave the culprits who nailed His hands and feet to the cross. He couldn't physically walk free, but that didn't matter. In His heart and in His spirit, He kept himself free. In His spirit, He refused the enemy's spikes and He refused the enemy's chains. Had He refused to forgive His assailants, Jesus would have been bound to them and to Satan forever.

Sometimes the enemy puts you in a situation where you can't openly fight or walk away. God says, "I still left you with a weapon...your mouth." Your praise is your weapon. In those situations, God wants you to use your mouth and not your hands. Don't talk to the people who are persecuting you. Talk to God. Offer Him your praise. When you are in a situation where most would say a screaming fit is appropriate, offer God your praise instead. In some situations, the only person you can speak to is the Father.

So watch yourselves. If your brother sins, rebuke him, and if he repents, forgive him. If he sins against you seven times in a day, and seven times comes back to you and says, "I repent," forgive him.

—Luke 17:3-4

Some people have a big problem with repeat offenders— those people in your life who keep on offending and then come back to ask forgiveness. Others find it difficult to pray for those who truly are working to destroy them.

If you find it difficult to pray for your enemies, remember this. What they did on purpose helped you get to your purpose. Paul admonished the Philippians in *"Rejoice in the Lord always." (Philippians 4:4)* And James tells us to, *"Consider it pure joy, my brothers, whenever you face trials of many kinds, because you know that the testing of your faith develops perseverance." (James 1:2-3)* God has put his Holy Spirit in you. If you have His Spirit then you have His fruit—self-control. You have authority over your emotions. Humankind may have lost its authority over the Garden of Eden, but the work of Christ has restored our authority over emotions. The Holy Spirit resides in you to make that authority a reality in your daily life.

One week after Hurricane Katrina I was invited to be a part of a group to go to the devastated Gulf Coast and see what America's media called "refugees." These were my brothers and sisters who were live in isolated in Houston. I walked in and saw babies with no diapers. I met men who felt emasculated because they couldn't provide for their children. I saw grandmothers who were vulnerable because they now had to shower in public places. I was angry with America for not stepping up to the plate. I was angry with the church for not opening its doors. I was angry with civil rights organizations for not having a louder voice.

Then in a quiet moment, the still, small voice of the Holy Spirit helped me realize that anger was not a remedy either.

What benefit would it have been for me to write a scary letter to the President? How would it have helped me to burn down the stadium in Houston? None of that would change any of the circumstances in the devastated areas. A response like that would only change my circumstance—and change it for the worse. I had no desire to do something so rash that would place me in jail.

Our team came back home, and within four weeks raised a hundred thousand dollars. We put our energy into action instead of anger. With the money, we were able to send help to the churches that were devastated. We gave toward the historically black colleges that were ruined and we gave a hand to family members who had relocated to our pastoral jurisdiction. In doing that, I converted my anger into energy. That was made possible when I surrendered my anger to the Holy Spirit.

So many of us wrongly use our anger, and we pay the consequence for it in our bodies and in our physical circumstances. Sitting in jail for hitting your spouse is a waste of your time and theirs. Nothing good can come from it. You lose your job or your family, and you hand over control of at least a portion of your future to a judge, rather than to God. Not to mention the hurt and pain you cause to everyone who knows you.

God allows anger to come our way so we can be motivated toward the action He desires. Not so we can vent our emotions in a rage. Not so we can vindicate ourselves at a cost to everyone around us. He wants us to take the energy aroused by that emotion and translate it into fuel to change our circumstances. That's what the whole "fight or flight" thing is about. God put that emotion in you for a purpose, but He wants you to control it. That's part of the reason why He gave you the Holy Spirit.

★

So many of us wrongly use our anger, and we pay the consequence for it in our bodies and in our physical circumstances.

★

Whatever angers you ought to ignite you to do something powerful, penetrating, and perpetual. If what is upsets you is not propelling you to change, then you are not angry, you are just vengeful. When you get angry, don't think about punching someone or breaking something. Get by yourself, ask the Holy Spirit to show you the source of your anger, and then ask Him to show you constructive ways to change the cause.

The fight that you are in right now is a very critical and pivotal one. Right now you are in a fight that will determine who controls you. You are fighting because there are so many entities trying to manipulate you, trying to handle you, trying to push you, but the Lord wants to give you control of your emotions.

You aren't the first person to be manipulated by a competitor, a spouse, a friend, or an employer. People have been getting the bait and switch for a long time. Their attempts to maneuver you into agreeing with their terms or engaging them on their battlefield are nothing new. They just want to lure you into a position where your efforts complement and contribute to what they are doing. No employer has ever hired anyone in order to make that person rich. Your employer didn't hire you to make you rich. He hired you to make him rich.

You are fighting to get back control of your life. There are people who thought they had control over you, over what you do and how your gift expands your prosperity. God has a different plan. By the presence of his Holy Spirit in you, He is handing back the reigns of your emotions, of your life. There are people who think you are not going to be a success without them, people who think the only way you'll going to make it is if you connect to them. Your emotions are a key element in their attempts to manipulate and maintain control over you. This is an attempt to commandeer your destiny. God will never let that happen. You can't cooperate with their attempts. You have to exercise the self-control God has already planted in you through His Spirit. Not only are you going to control yourself, you are going to control the opponent.

One of the greatest boxers was Muhammad Ali. In his fight against Joe Frazier, many of the boxing critics thought Ali was going to go down because he was not a traditional fighter. Ali boxed with his hands down near his waist as a technique to get his opponent close. And when he got his adversary close, he was fast enough to strike in the place of greatest vulnerability. He spent much of the fight near the ropes, dancing on the balls of his feet all the way around the ring.

The opponent would spend his energy trying to cut off Ali's movement. When the opponent succeeded, Ali would sag against the ropes, cover his face with his hands, and catch his breath. While the opponent pounded his fists against Ali's shoulders and arms, Ali was regaining his strength. Regardless of how it might have appeared to those in attendance, or those watching on television, the opponent didn't control him. He controlled the opponent.

Controlling your opponent takes you into an area of spiritual warfare where the risk seems to get a bit higher. This is essentially what God did with Satan.

Satan thought he was in control. He'd been tossed out of heaven and landed on earth with a third of the angelic

151

host. On earth, he deceived mankind and took over man's authority. He might have realized there was one avenue through which God could take back authority. Having created man in His own image, God could become human without having to give up His divine nature. That image of God into which mankind was created provides a point of commonality between man and God. God isn't man. Man isn't God. But the commonality gave God an opening through which He could enter His created order on a human level and win back mankind's control over that creation.

Satan might have known this was a possibility. If he did, I doubt he ever thought God would actually do it. When the incarnation occurred and Jesus appeared, Satan knew God had entered the created order as a human. He might have thought God was going to establish His earthly, physical kingdom right then. But when Jesus was nailed to the cross, things looked different. I'm sure Satan thought he was still in control—until the resurrection. When Jesus came up from the tomb, Satan knew it was over.

Until the resurrection, the fight looked like Satan was in control. Jesus was on the ropes. In reality, He was just waiting for the right moment. When that moment came, Jesus dropped a left hook.

The authority God gave Adam in the Garden now has been restored to you. You have the authority to give to Satan the same command Jesus gave to him, "Be quiet, and go away." You don't have to shout it. You don't have to stomp your foot and growl. Instead of shouting in anger at whoever is confronting you, instead of letting your emotions run wild, quietly turn from them to your spiritual enemy and calmly say, "Be quiet, and go away."

Jesus has returned authority to you. The Holy Spirit's presence in your life puts you in control.

To regain your control, you have to complicate your issue. People have to know it is not just one thing you are going through; it is a whole buffet. The devil puts all his energy into the small issues while your mind is still on the bigger picture. You might lose some battles, but you'll still win the war. God says, "With all the issues, with all the drama, with all the things going on in your life, I want you to stay focused on your purpose. It doesn't matter what else is going on in your life. As long as you stay focused on your purpose, it doesn't matter what's going to happen." The enemy in his autobiography is the author of confusion. You can't be mad at the enemy when he is doing his job. He is supposed to bring confusion to your life. The only way you are going to win is if you confuse the confuser. When you are confusing him, he will throw whatever trouble he can into your lap. You are then going to take that and confuse him. For example, when you lose your job, and he

> ★
>
> *The enemy in his autobiography is the author of confusion. You can't be mad at the enemy when he is doing his job. He is supposed to bring confusion to your life.*
>
> ★

slithers away thinking he's gotten you on the run, confuse him. How? The next morning, get up, put your suit on, get your briefcase, and start walking like you are going to work. Confuse the confuser. When you are frustrated, praise God more. When you are broke, God has your back. Thank God for His provision and look as though you have no financial concerns. When you don't allow your lack of funds to dictate how you carry yourself, you've confused the confuser. You will win this war on the element of surprise. If you do the unexpected, you will get the unexpected.

Chapter 13

I AM THE WEAPON
OF GOD

★

You are my war club, my weapon for battle—with You I destroy kingdoms, with You I shatter chariot and driver...

—Jeremiah 51:20-21

Joseph, one of the heroes of the patriarchal narratives in the book of Genesis, was Jacob's eleventh son. He was sold into slavery as a young boy by his brothers who were jealous of his dreams and envious of the favor their father showed him—favor made evident by the coat of many colors Jacob had given him. A coat they saw every day.

Like Daniel, Joseph had a gift that took him to the heights of power. And, like Daniel, that gift was the ability to interpret dreams. It took Joseph a while to understand it, though. At first, he thought receiving dreams was the extent of the gift. Those dreams were just the first manifestation of the gift. The full manifestation included the ability to interpret the dreams for others. Having dreams with meaning for his own life benefited himself. Being able to interpret the dreams of others benefited someone else.

> *Your gift—that special ability and calling you received from God— was given to you for the purpose of blessing the people around you.*

Your gift—that special ability and calling you received from God—was given to you for the purpose of blessing the people around you. It's a Kingdom gift. It was given to you and through you for the benefit of the Kingdom of God.

Joseph had the ability to interpret dreams, but he received favor before he received the dreams. Joseph's father doted on him more than he did all of his other sons. The dreams came after he received the coat of many colors. That coat was like a symbol of the bestowing of his gift—like Elisha receiving Elijah's mantle as a symbol of the anointing he received at Elijah's death.

Joseph didn't realize it but at that very moment he became a powerful tool. He became a weapon in God's hands. When

Joseph added obedience to that gift, he became a formidable force. That anointing, that favor he received gave him the potential to achieve great success. It also sent a signal that attracted the enemy.

In modern warfare, armies use radar to detect enemy aircraft. That same radar guides the antiaircraft missiles to the enemy planes. It's very effective. However, radar works by sending out a signal that bounces off objects in the sky and returns to a receiver on the ground. Once they turn on the radar system, that signal acts like a retractor beam guiding enemy aircraft straight toward the antiaircraft units. In Desert Storm, the Iraqi military learned very quickly that turning on their radar systems was the quickest way to give away their location. After the first day, they didn't turn them on anymore.

> ★
>
> *Joseph was not attacked by strangers, but by his own family. There is no greater pain than the pain of being hurt by your own family*
>
> ★

The anointing you receive will grant you favor from God. It will also draw an attack from the enemy. That's because the anointing makes you a powerful weapon in the Kingdom of God. As I've said before, any move toward God brings opposition from Satan. Once you receive favor from God, the enemy redoubles his attack.

Joseph had a dream, and when he told it to his brothers, they hated him all the more.
—Genesis 37:5

Joseph was not attacked by strangers, but by his own family. There is no greater pain than the pain of being hurt by your own family—a family that can't see your gift and don't like your dream. They don't realize you are called out, separated, and different from everyone else. Even if they do, they don't like it. Joseph's own family attacked him and threw him in a pit. From that pit, Joseph was elevated into slavery. It's tough to think of slavery as a step up, but for Joseph it was much better than the alternative. Sometimes elevation leads you into isolation. When he was pulled out from the pit, he thought he was being rescued. As it turned out, he was, but not before things got worse. Being sold into slavery was better than dying in that well, but when they pulled him out I'm sure he thought they were going to send him home to his father. Instead, they sent him off to a foreign country. Being alive and enslaved at the same time is a double pain.

While in slavery, Joseph's circumstances took a turn for the worse. He found himself falsely accused of rape and put in jail.

After being in jail a while, Joseph had two cell mates from Pharoah's court—a baker and a cupbearer. The Bible doesn't tell us what they did wrong to put them in jail. We do not even know their names but they are identified by their gift. One a baker, the other a cupbearer. People will know you by your gift too. They don't need to know your name. Your gift will make room for you.

God could have put a thief or a murderer in the cell with Joseph. Instead, He arranged for a baker and a cupbearer. Joseph had a gift. For that gift to take him where God wanted him to go, Joseph had to connect with someone else's gift. That someone was Pharoah's cupbearer. Joseph is remembered for his dreams and his ability to interpret the dreams of others. But his gift concerning dreams would have gone no further than his own amusement had he not connected with the cupbearer's gift. Through the cupbearer's gift, Joseph was connected to people of influence. Time spent with the cupbearer, opened doors of opportunity for Joseph. Those doors took Joseph to great success. The cupbearer was as much a part of what God did through Joseph as was Joseph himself.

No one extols the virtues of the cupbearer, but we could make a very good point by telling this story from his perspective. As I said, the cupbearer's name is not mentioned in the Genesis account. Still, the story would not have worked out the way it did had he not used his gift and allowed that gift to take him to his destiny. Having done that, we might suppose he was a man who didn't care whether his name appeared in the book of Genesis. He didn't receive an award. He didn't need one. He didn't need a certificate or a trophy. All he needed was to exercise his gift. That gift put him in a place of opportunity. He recognized the importance of his position, and made the most of it. By learning to recognize the opportunity for what it was, he was also able to see the possibilities available for others. Walking in his God-given position paired those opportunities with the people around him opening doors for the others' gifts to take them to their destiny as well.

That's going farther with the cupbearer's story than Scripture takes it, but you see my point. God orchestrates people and a variety of circumstances to get you to a place where your gift can accelerate. That makes you a very valuable and powerful weapon in His arsenal. It also makes you a really big target for the enemy, regardless of whether you are the king or the king's cupbearer.

Then the chief cupbearer said to Pharaoh, 'Today I am reminded of my shortcomings. Pharaoh was once angry with his servants and he imprisoned me and the chief baker in the house of the captain of the guard. Each of us had a dream the same night, and each dream had a meaning of its own. Now a young Hebrew was there with us, a servant of the captain of the guard. We told him our dreams, and he interpreted them for us, giving each man the interpretation of his dream. And things turned out exactly as he interpreted them to us: I was restored to my position, and the other man was hanged. So Pharaoh sent for Joseph, and he was quickly brought from the dungeon. When he had shaved and changed his clothes, he came before Pharaoh. Pharaoh said to Joseph, "I had a dream, and no one can interpret it. But I have heard it said of you that when you hear a dream you can interpret it."

—Genesis 41:9–15

Joseph was destined for greatness. God had given him a gift that would take him there. He had anointed him with favor that would open doors for him. Still, Joseph had to make the connection to that destiny. In our human space-time continuum, here in this life as God has created it to be, in life as we know it, that connection usually requires a human-to-human relationship. Joseph had to connect with a person whose gift could match up everything. Real events had to transpire in real time. That connection came for Joseph, but it didn't take a route that human thought would label logical.

We in our Western mind-set expect things to happen in a linear manner. Joseph– favor– gift– introduction– success. That's not how it works—not usually. There are other dynamics involved—other people and the opposition—that all worked together to produce a much different route for Joseph to follow his gift to his destiny. That route took twists and turns because Satan did his best to prevent Joseph from reaching his destiny. Joseph, armed with a gift, blessed with favor, connected to his station, would be a powerful warrior in the hands of God. The enemy couldn't let that happen. The really wonderful thing is, the enemy can't stop it from happening. All those twists and turns—the pit into which his brothers threw him, Potiphar's house, prison—were obstacles thrown up by Satan to prevent Joseph's success. God took every one of those obstacles and used them to reveal, clarify, hone, and perfect the gift in Joseph. What others thought would destroy Joseph, God used to make him the man He wanted him to be all along.

For most people, prison is not the last stop before dinner with the king. Prison is the last stop before the graveyard. In American culture today, prison is a mark on a person's life that squelches opportunity. For Joseph, prison was the key to the fulfillment of his destiny.

If you're stuck someplace that looks like one of those career-ending holes, take heart. God is not limited by the limitations people create for one another. Regardless of what you face right now, you are still a mighty weapon in God's hands. Brokenness is not a bad thing in the kingdom of God. Brokenness only means your personality is no longer an obstacle to God's complete use of you. When Paul struggled with this very issue, he received a word from the Lord in 2 Corinthians 12:9: *My grace is sufficient for you, for my power is made perfect in weakness.* Your weakness is your greatest strength because that weakness opens you up to the grace of God. Through that grace, His power can be made evident in your life. That power is the warrior's power you need for the battles that lie ahead.

> *You have favor on your life and a dream that has not yet come to pass.*

Before Joseph went to prison, he thought his gift was the receiving of dreams. It took prison for him to find out his gift was much bigger. His real gift was the interpretation of dreams. He didn't know what his real gift was until he was stuck in a place from which he could not extract himself. Satan had him in that jail, thinking Joseph was out of the way and no longer a threat. Little did he know that was the very place God wanted him to be. Satan put Joseph there because he was a great weapon of God who wanted him there for the very same reason. Joseph had to learn the extent of his gift. After all, it wasn't the dreams that took him into Pharaoh's court but the interpretations.

God is going to unveil to you what your real gift is and what you were created to do. He is going to reveal to you what you were born to accomplish. You have favor on your life and a dream that has not yet come to pass. Understand that in order to cause your path to cross with your connection to the place God has ordained for you, you may have to endure something as harsh as Joseph endured. Your gift makes you a weapon for God, but you are His weapon. He knows best how to use you and where to apply your gift. Yield to Him and let Him set you up in the place from which your gift can be used by Him to project His power. Your gift is not for your benefit alone. It is a Kingdom gift. It was given to you by the King of kings to benefit His kingdom. And since God is ruler of this Kingdom, He gets the final word on where and how that gift is employed.

As iron sharpens iron, so one man sharpens another.

—Proverbs 27:17

In order for you to be fully operational in your gift, a weapon that He can use, God has to sharpen you. He has to put an edge on you. To do that, God will move you into relationships with people who can refine and hone that gift. Those relationships may not be the easy, friendly ones you desire.

Rubbing shoulders with people who are excited about being successful in the Lord puts you in contact with people who can open doors for you. It also puts you in contact with people the enemy is bent on destroying. You cannot fight this fight alone. You need to surround yourself with a small group of people who are not threatened by your destiny or jealous of the success that opens before you.

Every warrior called of God reaches a point in life where circumstances conspire to make him or her feel insignificant and devoid of value. This is a painful process, but at that lowest point God is able to strip away pride, self esteem, and love for oneself. That stripping away is much like boot camp. When a person enlists in the military they don't go straight into war. First, they go through boot camp. There, they are driven through a training process that lasts several months. During that process, the civilian perspective is stripped from that individual. In its place, drill instructors build a warrior's perspective.

God takes you through that same process. You come to your gift with certain expectations and presumptions, an attitude you learned from the life you lived to that point. When you surrender to God, He takes you through a process of "unlearning" all those attitudes. Those wrong attitudes and incorrect assumptions keep you from understanding the full extent of your gift. They keep you from being completely useful to God and hinder the complete manifestation of your gift. Yield to that work of the Holy Spirit in your life. Let Him have unhindered access to the deepest parts of your mind, will, emotions, and spirit. He knows where your gift will take you. He wants you to reach that place even more than you do. You are a warrior, a weapon in the hands of God. With you, He can break down strongholds and defeat empires. With you He can conquer lands and liberate the oppressed. You have to let Him teach you how to be that warrior.

Not long ago I attended a For Men Only conference in Dallas, Texas, hosted by Bishop T.D. Jakes. Among the speakers was Bishop Eddie Long, pastor of New Birth Church in Decatur, Georgia. He shared his testimony of how in the darkest moment of his life, he was about to commit a double homicide and suicide. He was at odds with his wife and had come to a day when he was prepared to kill his wife and child and then turn the gun on himself. He went home with a loaded gun under the seat of his car. When he walked into the house, his wife and child already had moved out. He began to cry and thank God. Had they been there that day, he would now be either dead or waiting for his turn on death row.

The time for playing around has passed. This warfare is real. Satan isn't interested in taking prisoners. He wants to take you out. He's not playing for the fun of it. This is a life-and-death struggle. You may find yourself in situations where you are the only thing standing between those around you and death. You may be the only one who sees the attack for what it truly is. Draw your sword! Raise your shield! Proclaim the Word of the Lord and speak His Word into your circumstances. He is powerful, and He is powerful through you.

You are my war club, my weapon for battle— with You I shatter nations, with You I destroy kingdoms...

—Jeremiah 51:20

All God needs to accomplish His will; all He needs to obtain victory in battle, is you. You are his battle ax. You are a registered weapon with God. In you resides the power of the Holy Spirit—the power that created the universe, the power that parted the Red Sea, the power that resurrected and glorified Jesus. That same power resides in you. You have the power to say to the lame, "Stand up and walk," and see it come to pass. That power is the power of the Holy Spirit.

That same power can break down strongholds of oppression and bigotry. If we understood the power of the Holy Spirit that dwells in us, we could transform our nation. Dr. Martin Luther King, Jr., caught a glimpse of that power. We can take up that cause. The enemy will use anything to stop us from reaching our destiny—racism, bigotry, ignorance. We have to fight against that. Marches, protests, and picket lines are just as much a part of this warfare as prayer and fasting. This war in which we are engaged is waged in the heavens and right here on Earth. Don't waste your efforts on fighting for cars, houses, and jewelry. This fight is about shifting nations. We have the opportunity to participate in real change. We have access to the power that can transform this nation. Don't let Satan divert you into battling over useless material goods that in the end make no difference to anyone.

If My people who are called by My name will humble themselves and pray and seek My face and turn from their wicked ways, then will I hear from heaven and will forgive their sins and heal their land.

—2 Chronicles 7:14

Through you, God will shift kingdoms and bless third-world nations. When you yield your gift to God you influence other areas with consequences and blessings of which you may not be aware. Your obedience might unlock healing for three hundred eighty-five million people with HIV/AIDS in Africa. A seemingly chance conversation with a stranger might put in motion events that release aid for the people in Sudan. God is capable of using you not just for your community but to change the world. To enter into that work you have to learn to listen with your spirit to that still, small voice from the Holy Spirit.

God has chosen to use you to destroy demonic kingdoms. He has positioned you to fight against demons and command them to return to where they came from. Whatever the devil fortified, God will demolish through you. The weapons of God are mighty for the pulling down of strongholds and the building up of nations. (2 Corinthians 10:4) You can see that in Joseph's life.

Like Joseph to his generation, so was Dr. Martin Luther King Jr. to the twentieth century. Dr. King was a gifted man.

Joseph's gift—his ability to hear the voice of the Holy Spirit as He gave the interpretation of Pharaoh's dream—elevated Joseph to a position of power and influence. He used that power to administer the lands of all of Egypt. Through his office, he orchestrated the collection of grain from the harvest for the next seven years. At the end of those first seven years a famine struck Egypt. The grain reserve Joseph created fed all of Egypt during that famine. It also fed Joseph's own family, including those brothers who had sold him into slavery.

Had Joseph yielded to the attacks of the enemy, ignored God, and allowed himself to become bitter and resentful over the events that transpired earlier in his life, he would never have reached that meeting with Pharaoh. He would never have been in a position to interpret Pharaoh's dream. The gift would have been wasted on trifling amusement when it could have been used to save and transform a nation. Your gift is no less critical.

Like Joseph to his generation, so was Dr. Martin Luther King Jr. to the twentieth century. Dr. King was a gifted man. God bestowed on him gifts of leadership, discernment, and courage. Not only that, he was an intelligent man with an oratorical gift and a quick mind. He could have been a seminary professor or pastor of his father's church, a noted Bible scholar or a successful author. He also could have allowed the events of his life to make him bitter, resentful, and angry. Instead, he yielded to God and allowed himself to become a weapon in His hands. He refused to settle for the average life, and he refused to allow Satan to divert him from God's appointed destiny. Because of that, the grip of this nation's racial legacy was finally pried loose from our throat.

As the Honorable Benjamin A. Gilman said on the floor of the United States Congress, "Dr. King contributed more to the causes of national freedom and equality than any other individual of the twentieth century. His achievements as an author and as a minister were surpassed only by his leadership, which transformed a torn people into a beacon of strength and solidarity, and united a divided nation under a common creed of brotherhood and mutual prosperity."

That is a description of a man anointed by God, a man elevated to a position of influence by his gift. God isn't just interested in transforming you, your family, or your neighborhood. He is interested in transforming and changing the world. You are a warrior in that cause. In His hands, you can be the weapon He uses to bring to pass His vision for all of humanity. In His hands, you can be the instrument that leads us all to the victory and destiny God has ordained.

Chapter 14

PRAYER IS IN MY ARSENAL

———————————★———————————

Watch and pray so that you will not fall into temptation.

—Matthew 26:41

Anyone who has ever been around me for any length of time can tell you I am a professional talker. Resting in silence is a constant battle for me. Many of you have that same struggle. The discipline of silence is difficult to achieve in the communicative society in which we live. Television is everywhere. Radio is always accessible, and with satellite radio you can listen to almost any broadcast program in the country. Books and music are available on tape and CD, and if you don't like it that way, you can download it to a player so small it will fit inside a clinched fist. We are constantly bombarded by communication. We're reared, trained, and educated in the art of communicating. This aspect of our socialization has deep spiritual consequences. Most of us are good talkers, but poor listeners.

In his book, *The Five Love Languages,* Dr. Gary Chapman addresses communication between spouses. Listening is a gift. Most couples find themselves at odds with each other because they both talk and express themselves, but they rarely hear what the other is saying.

Early in my ministry I traveled every week, sometimes almost every day, preaching the Gospel. That schedule took a heavy toll on my marriage. My former wife complained bitterly about how I never spent time with her. In response, I bought her gifts while on the road—dresses, books, perfumes, jewelry—thinking that those gifts would compensate for my absence. As you might expect, she made it clear she would rather have tarnished jewelry and an old dress if that would get me home to her. I kept traveling. We kept arguing. Then one day it finally dawned on me; I hadn't been listening. I thought she would be happy with presents, but what she really wanted was my presence.

In prayer most of us make the same mistake I made in marriage. We become entrenched in the business of life—working, going to school, raising our family. All too easily we become career-oriented and finance-occupied while God is beckoning, "I don't just want your attention on Sunday. I want to commune with you on Monday through Saturday too."

If asked, most believers would profess to have a prayer life. They pray three times a day: before meals, at night before bed, when bad news has been delivered, or when having trouble with one of their children. Few make prayer a daily discipline. Fewer still sit long enough to hear God speak to them, allowing Him to examine their hearts and lives.

Elijah was greatly used of God, but he too, had to be reminded of the importance of listening. He had just succeeded at Mt. Carmel, when he'd called upon the name of the Lord and fire came down from heaven and burnt his offering. The people of Israel turned their hearts back to worshiping God instead of worshiping Baal. Elijah's ministry set the people of Israel in the right direction. It made the wicked queen Jezebel angry. She sent Elijah a message in 1 Kings 19:2 that she intended to have him killed *by tomorrow about this time.* Elijah knew how ruthless she could be and surrendered to the fear her message stirred in his heart. He fled for his life into the wilderness. There, he hid in a cave.

God was gentle in restoring Elijah to faith. He passed by the cave where Elijah was hid, and a great and strong whirlwind rent the mountain and broke the rocks to pieces. But God was not in the whirlwind. After the whirlwind, an earthquake shook the ground, and after the quake came a great fire. God was not in those, either. Then after the fire came a gentle whisper. When Elijah heard it, he went out and stood at the entrance of the cave. *And the voice came to him saying, "What are you doing here, Elijah?"* (1 Kings 19:13).

It wasn't until after the whirlwind, the earthquake, the fire, that the voice came to Elijah. Not a great, booming, well-modulated voice, but a still, small voice—a whisper. Elijah's ears had to be tuned to the Spirit of God in order for him to hear it. He had to be listening.

In the business of life, we have to learn not only to bombard God with our wants and needs, but also to be silent before Him and listen for that still, small voice. What God has to say to you is far more important than what you have to say to Him. He knows the future. He knows your identity. He knows from which direction the enemy will attack. He knows the response that will send the enemy running. You need to listen to God so He can tell you.

★

In the business of life, we have to learn not only to bombard God with our wants and needs, but also to be silent before Him and listen for that still, small voice.

★

There is a story about a Native American visiting New York City for the first time. This Native American was walking through the city alongside a native New Yorker. Suddenly, the first-time visitor turned to his companion and said excitedly, "I hear a cricket." Astonished, the New Yorker asked, "How is it possible for you to hear a cricket with all of the traffic and noise?" "Well," the visitor replied, "I'm not listening for the sound of traffic or all those other things. I am listening for the sound of nature." Likewise, we ought to tune out the sounds from the things around us and tune in to the sound of God's voice.

One of my favorite personalities in the Bible is the prophet Daniel. In the third year of Jehoiakim's reign as king of Judah, the Babylonians attacked Jerusalem. They plundered the city, took whatever they found, rounded up the best and brightest of Judah's citizens, and carried them off to Babylon. Daniel was one of those taken captive. He and three of his friends, Shadrach, Meshach, and Abednego, were tested by Nebuchadnezzar, the king of Babylon. When he found they highly were intelligent, he took them into his service. Until Nebuchadnezzar died, Daniel served him faithfully.. When King Cyrus succeeded Nebuchadnezzar, Daniel was relegated to the ranks of the unemployed.

Daniel was a long way from home—far from the friends and relatives around whom he'd lived all his life. He had been trained in the disciplines of the Jewish faith, to love and serve the Lord. In Babylon, far from his beloved Jerusalem, he was surrounded by pagans—pagan gods, pagan women, pagan practices. No doubt, he had many surrounding him urging that he to adopt the local customs. Things might have gone much smoother for him if he had. Daniel wasn't interested in the easy route. He was more concerned with pleasing God than with giving in to the pressures of local culture. So, he resisted

One of the disciplines Daniel determined in his heart to remain faithful to the strict adherence to Jewish dietary law. He and his companions refused to eat anything but vegetables. The other discipline he followed was the discipline of prayer. We don't think too much about prayer as a discipline anymore. Even in strong churches prayer is thought of in a casual way. It's true we should pray without ceasing and learn to view prayer as an attitude that permeates our lifestyle. Still, concerted, regular prayer—time alone with God when there is nothing around to distract you or interrupt you—is one of the most powerful disciplines of the Christian faith. Daniel practiced the discipline of prayer. (Daniel 1:8-16)

There they were, Daniel and his friends, a long way from home, yet they held to that discipline. And it's good they did.

In the second year of his reign, Nebuchadnezzar had an unsettling dream. He called his magicians together and asked them to tell him what the dream meant. They were eager to oblige and asked him to tell them the dream. Nebuchadnezzar refused. He had come to suspect that the magicians told him whatever they thought he wanted to hear. This time, things would be different. This time, he told them to tell him both the dream and the interpretation. They thought he was crazy. The king was serious—deadly serious. He issued a decree that if the magicians could not tell him both the dream and the interpretation he would kill them all. They were unable to do it, so he issued a decree to have them put to death.

When Daniel found out they were all to be executed, including himself and his friends, he asked the king to delay their execution to allow him time to intercede with God. The king agreed. *Then Daniel returned to his house and explained the matter to his friends ... He urged them to plead for mercy from the God of heaven concerning this mystery, so that he and his friends might not be executed with the rest of the wise men of Babylon* (Daniel 2:18-19). In short, Daniel and his friends prayed. That night, God gave him the answer.

The next day, Daniel told the king his dream and gave him the interpretation. He had obtained that information from God through prayer. As a result, Daniel and his friends were made administrators over all of Babylon. Through prayer, Daniel and his three friends moved from servants in the court of the king to running the daily operation of the empire. Prayer shifted them from servant to commander. They attained that blessing through prayer. Not just a few words while they were busy at some other task, but by an unwavering commitment to the discipline of prayer. I'm not suggesting you can manipulate God. I am simply saying, disciplined prayer takes you deeper into the heart of God and allows Him to go deeper into your heart. The depth of that relationship makes a big difference in how far your gift can take you.

According to Daniel 1:17, Daniel had the gift of interpreting dreams from the very beginning. That ability was a gift from God. How far Daniel could go with that gift, how far that gift could take him, depended on how much God could get of Daniel and how much Daniel could get of God. To do that, God had to go deep into Daniel's heart. Daniel had to go deep into God's heart. That process, that journey of going deeper, is a process and journey taken through prayer—disciplined, regular, deep prayer. Pouring out your heart—the good, the bad, the nasty, the ugly—in selfless transparency before God.

When you surrender at that level, when you open up to Him, He opens up to you.

Many people wonder why someone else has gone so much farther than they have. They see someone whose gift has taken them from insurmountable lows to unbelievable heights. Some who see that are jealous and filled with envy. The reason for the difference is grace, but it is grace poured out through a response to grace. God offers you grace, you respond to it. God pours out more. If you stop somewhere along the way, God stops. The extent of how far your gift can take you is limited only by how far into yourself you are willing to let God have access and how far into Him you are willing to go. If you don't stop, God won't stop.

When you start praying like that, Satan will throw up some serious roadblocks in your path. You won't believe the lengths to which he'll go to keep you from following that kind of discipline.

As your prayer time approaches, you'll be tired. The children will need help with homework. Your wife will want to talk. Your parents will drop by. A friend will call to talk.

The farther you go, the more serious the obstacles will become. The car will break down. Money will get tight. You'll have to take a second job. All kinds of stuff will break out on you. Don't give up on that discipline. The discipline alone, in and of itself, doesn't do anything. This isn't magic—bow and say some words and things happen. No. It's not like that. But it's not like doing nothing either.

The discipline of prayer is your discipline. It's something for you and for your benefit. God can accomplish His purposes in the world with or without you. You need this kind of prayer. You need your gift to take you to places unknown. The discipline of prayer is first for your good, and through that to the Kingdom and purposes of God.

Don't give up on the discipline of prayer.

Now, there's another interesting thing about prayer in the book of Daniel.

Later on in his life, kings had come and gone and Daniel was pretty much forgotten by everyone—except God. In the third year of Cyrus, Daniel received a word from God. That word told him things about a war that was to come. Daniel did not fully understand what that word meant, so he prayed for understanding. And he prayed. And he prayed some more. He prayed for twenty-four days. Finally, on the twenty-fourth day, an angel appeared to him to tell him what the vision meant.

> ★
>
> *Don't give up on the discipline of prayer.*
>
> ★

The angel said in Daniel 10:12–14, *Do not be afraid, Daniel. Since the first day that you set your mind to gain understanding and to humble yourself before God, your words were heard, and I have come in response to them. But the prince of the Persian kingdom resisted me twenty-one days. Then Michael, one of the chief princes, came to help me ..."*

This is a very interesting description. The person talking to Daniel was an angel. He told Daniel that his prayers were heard from the first day he prayed and help was dispatched that very day, but that help was opposed. There is a war raging in heaven—a war that affects the delivery of answers to prayer. This is serious business. Prayer is not just a nice, quiet activity reserved for a group of elderly ladies who gather at the church on Thursdays for tea and cake and a few minutes with God. Prayer is part of that readiness fitted on your feet that Paul describes in Ephesians 6:15. He mentions it in regard to your feet because it is your prayers that put feet to God's answers. Your prayers invite God into the human space-time continuum.

Prayer is an essential weapon of the spiritual warriors of this age. You can see from the description in Daniel, your prayers have a direct effect in the supernatural realm. They link you with angels and archangels and with all the company of heaven.

What the angel told Daniel should wipe away any doubt you may have had that we are engaged in a war. The delay Daniel experienced in receiving an answer to his prayer wasn't because of God's refusal to answer. On the contrary, it was because there was a fierce battle against that answer to keep Daniel from receiving it.

Some of you think you have not received an answer to your prayers because God refuses to answer or because He isn't paying attention. Nothing could be farther from the truth. God has already dispatched the answer to your prayers. The delay is due to the opposition thrown up by Satan. He is *not* a coequal with God, but he can delay those answers. That is why the discipline of prayer is so essential. Don't give up. Press on through.

My call to become a pastor was strange. I was thriving in ministry and I had just spoken at the NAACP national convention in 1999 when my former wife came up to me and said, "This season in your life is over. You no longer challenge and you no longer stretch." And I started to feel the call to become a pastor. The bishop over California jurisdiction told me about Bryant Temple AME church and that there was an opening because the pastor there was up in age and said he wanted me to be his successor and asked if I was interested. Though this was God speaking, I packed my things and moved to California, but the pastor decided not to retire. I came back home. Two weeks later the bishop from Florida called and said he had heard what had happened in California and that he would have a church open. I went there and preached, came back home, and slipped into depression. A graduate of Morehouse College, Duke Divinity School, grandson of a bishop, on the national stage for civil rights, and I could not get a church? Not every opportunity is God ordained. I felt like I did not want to preach again. I felt like church had not supported me and locked every door. My former wife who was my girlfriend at the time told me to start a church. The irony was that she was born and raised differently than me, so she had never witnessed a church plant. But what she said resonated something in my spirit, and I began to pray with intention. It wasn't until I stopped talking that I heard God say out of the silence, "Merge what you did in civil rights with a spiritual life." Out of the silence I could hear the Lord say, Empowerment Temple.

SECTION III

Chapter 15

GUERILLA WARFARE

★

If you have the faith, God has got the power.

In the year 2000 I had the distinct honor opportunity and humbling experience of serving as the campaign manager for one who would soon become the first woman elected bishop in the African Methodist Episcopal church. It was a difficult fight, an awesome and humbling experience. There were more than seventy-three candidates, and only three slots were available. It became extremely difficult as gender discrimination began to show itself in religion. Many people who lived within our region and jurisdiction wanted to stand against my candidate, not because she wasn't suited, trained, or able to produce but simply because of her gender. Many of those in power fought vigorously. They had larger churches with greater financial reservoirs to pull from and more political contacts. It looked as though we were coming up against an uphill battle. Even people who would have aligned with us took hold of a Nicodemus mentality—they would only support us under the cloak of darkness and in secrecy. We used as our theme, "It's now time."

How do you take that kind of assignment well knowing full well you don't have the resources, political backing, or public support? All you feel is that you are the best candidate for the job. You may be facing struggles at your job or school with every person seemingly stacked up against you, and the only thing that keeps you fighting is your understanding of your gift, the power of God, and potential the Lord has deposited in your heart.

> ★
>
> *Everybody wants to connect with a winner, but you have to have your strategy when your troops are still small, your resources minimal, but your faith is great.*
>
> ★

I came against a lot of resistance. Many people said to me, "Jamal, why would you risk yourself in helping a woman? She is going to fall short and tarnish you, yet you have a great career; more than that, you are a second-generation legacy. Your father is a bishop, your grandfather was a bishop. Why would you risk your career? Do something safe." But I knew I wasn't born, raised, or reared to play it safe. God created me to take risks.

Therefore, I took a risk on something I believed in and felt. Because I took this risk, my friends didn't understand me. The political allies didn't believe it simply because I had my own personal convictions. I fought through it like her campaign was my own.

On the first day of the elections, something that had never happened in the history of my denomination occurred. She earned more votes than ninety percent of the men who were running against her. Immediately when the numbers began to show themselves on the chart, people who weren't supporting us before began to jump the fence. It taught me a very valuable lesson. Everybody wants to connect with a winner, but you have to have your strategy when your troops are still small, your resources minimal, but your faith is great. We began to persevere and push forward, and on the night

Many of us are fighting through a battle that has been designed to break us, but will in fact enable us if we have the faith.

of the elections we elected through our leadership, faith, determination, and conviction, the first-ever elected woman bishop in the AME church. It was a historical moment, but it also was a lamp light for those who have to understand what guerrilla warfare looks like when you are not in a wildlife terrain.

Many of us are fighting through a battle that has been designed to break us, but will in fact enable us if we have the faith. I usually say, "If you have the faith, God has got the power." Most times when you are going through a battle, God always stacks the odds against you. It will seem as if you are fighting an entity that has more resources, more strength and finances, but the only way you are able to win is if you have more faith. You have to begin practicing guerrilla warfare, which in no uncertain terms helps you to understand that the greatest battle and greatest strategy begins with your mind. Because our mind was unbreakable, our campaigns were unshakable.

In 1947 the Japanese had imperialistic occupation over the entire nation of China. Mao Tse Tung wrote a book called *The Manual for Guerilla Warfare*. It was in its premise and introduction that guerilla warfare was necessary for every nation that does not have all the military strength as that for its opposing force; it has a smaller group, smaller base, and smaller finances. Guerilla warfare only takes place on the territory of the one who has been conquered. It is the entire aim of guerilla soldiers to regain the territory that has been lost. When the United States began to unleash an unprecedented battle fight in Iraq, it wasn't against the army of Iraq but rather against insurgence or what the Pentagon calls guerilla fighters.

Guerilla warfare to be defined is not about human beings but about political resources. It grows out of an environment that is unstable. It is a battle to influence the political mentality, and its target is not for mentality but it is for minds. The CIA when giving out its manual said, "If you are able to capture the mind, then you have already done more than a bullet."

What the enemy tries to do to the body of Christ is to kidnap our thinking. If the enemy is able to capture the mind then he has already conquered the terrain of our destiny. You have to know that the battle you are going through right now is a battle of your mind—a battle that will control how you think. If you start to think like you are defeated then your spirit will buy it and defeat will be yours for the taking. But when your mind reminds your spirit we are more than conquerors; when your mind takes on the understanding that *greater is He that is in me than the devil that is in the world;* (1 John 4:4)when you mind understands that we've got to win because *God is for us and who can be against us, (Romans 8:31)* then your victory is sure.

Because this is guerilla warfare, you have to know it is being launched against you and not by you. The enemy is unleashing guerilla tactics because he understands he has less power than you do; he understands he has less artillery than you; he understands he has less support than you do. You became more than a conqueror the very moment you decided to get saved; hence and you have more anointing in your fingertip than he has in his whole body. He is now trying to cause diversions to take you off your course.

Guerilla warfare usually takes place through surprise raids. It is never an act that is declared. So whenever there is a war that finds itself encroaching on your space—one you had not planned for—understand that the enemy is trying to unleash a surprise attack against you. That's why it is important that you remain sober of mind. Be ever ready. Until you enter your rest in heaven, you will always be on the devil's "hit list". Keep the following close to your heart: *will therefore bless the Lord at all times. His praise shall continually be on my lips* (Psalm 34:1), just so the enemy understands that I am in the combat position.

It is also intriguing to note that guerilla soldiers never dress in uniform. They come appearing to be civilians. They play the role of a friend and later manifest as foe. Some of the people you thought were friends are actually in place to dismantle that which God is try to building. If I can be of any encouragement in this; use wisdom when choosing your friends. You'll certainly find out who your real friends are when you are in the midst of a trial. It is easy to be friendly when life is good, but when the caves begin to crash in, friends become a rare jewel.

> ★
>
> *The enemy attacks you by bringing up something from your past, so that you will lose focus on the things that are in front of you.*
>
> ★

In dealing with guerilla warfare, you've got to understand that guerilla soldiers never attack from the front. They are trained to always hit from the rear, in so doing remove your focus from what is ahead. The enemy attacks you by bringing up something from your past, so that you will lose focus on the things that are in front of you. But Paul said, *Forgetting those things that are behind me, I press on towards the mark of the high calling* (Philippians 3:14). Guerillas never fight from upfront because they will never get upfront. The only way they can ever fight is from behind. You have to declare today you are healed from your past. Everything you went through is now behind you. As of this day, face what is ahead of you. The enemy will bring people from your past you didn't even know had your phone number, but when you start to see glimpses of your past then you can be certain your future is coming. The enemy wants to keep you strapped to your past because he already sees how bright your future is. God is getting ready to give you an overflow. He will give to you even what you do not need, just because your past was that bad and your future has to be that good.

The first objective of guerilla warriors is to cause disruption. The enemy wants to disrupt your schedule so you change your plan. Always ask yourself when faced with disruptions, "Is this an attempt to disrupt up my purpose? Could this interrupt the call of God on my life?" If you have no vision, you will have no interferences. Have you ever talked to somebody on the phone who has got nothing to do? They can talk to you for hours without disruption; but if you are talking to somebody who's got purpose, it won't be long before they say "hold on." If they are not important you will hang up, but if you need the information they've got, you will hold on till you get them on the line again. God says, "Even when I don't talk to you immediately, just hold on to the line and soon enough, you will hear my voice."

The second thing the enemy wants to bring during guerilla warfare after disruption is confusion. The enemy is the master of confusion. (James 3:16)He will throw all kinds of things on your lap so you don't even know what to focus on first. But when God has anointed you with a purpose and a vision, you've got to look past all of this and ask, "What is it in all of this that God is trying to show me?" When the enemy tries to confuse you, you've got to confuse him. When everything is tumbling all around, we can be certain that it isn't coming from God. We can put our hope and trust in Him. (1 Corinthians 14:33) I may have a lot of confusion in my life but one thing I am not confused about is God who woke me up this morning and put a vision in my heart. Everything around you can be a mess, vision can blur, but you can rest in the truth that God woke you in the morning and put the vision in your heart.

The third thing that guerillas want to do is to support the thing that opposes you. You know you have a guerilla in your camp when he is not affirming you but affirming your adversary. You've got to re-evaluate friends who are mad when you make progress or who act disappointed when you get elevation.

There are times when God will cause you to move into guerilla territory to propel you toward purpose and your supernatural success. Guerilla warriors would rather fight in a climate that is comfortable for them. They can get around easily. Choosing to only fight in their own territory makes it easier for them to maneuver and find vegetation and shelter. When they sense you crowding their space, you'll find your battle begin to intensify. You've encroached on their territory when you begin to dream bigger than what you did before or when you decide you're not settling for complacency any longer. If only you'd have been content to remain a prisoner, but moving out of that creates a threat and they must attack..Signs that you've stepped on his territory will show when you're suddenly out of a job, your relationship begins to unravel, or other major stressors hop into your lap. But be careful that you don't give too much credit to your adversary. He can do nothing unless he first has permission from God. Perhaps God is allowing this warfare to move you out of your safe little box and into the gifts and callings He created you for. God says, "I had to make the environment uncomfortable because only those who are anointed can handle conditions of any sort." Paul learned how to be abased and how to abound. It is easy to trust God when you are in an easy environment, but can you trust Him when you are in the harder times of your life too?

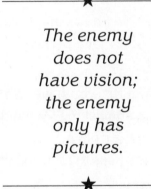

The enemy does not have vision; the enemy only has pictures.

Also, the guerillas need an area that is clear because they need high visibility with no technology. The enemy does not have vision; the enemy only has pictures. You have spent too much time trying to explain to visionless people your future, and you are trying to share with them what God has deposited in you, and they can't see it. You've got a vision other people can't see.

193

The US Army in its manual says, "In dealing with counter intelligence you've got to have METT-T." The M is mission. You've got to ask yourself in the middle of the battle, "Why is the enemy trying to stop my mission?" Take out the word *mission* and insert the word *purpose*. Why is the enemy trying to disrupt your purpose? Then ask yourself, "Why does my purpose upset the enemy?"

When you've got a purpose from God, that purpose is not to make you wealthy. Your purpose is always connected to having an impact. When it is a purpose given by God, it will not only bless you, but it will bless other people. So you've got to ask yourself, "Why is the devil trying to kill me?" He knows that if your purpose comes to pass, he can see how many people in your family are going to be shifted and changed.

Fourth, you have to ask, What weapon is the insurgent using against me? What does the enemy consistently use to delay me from getting to my purpose? Who is the person the enemy uses to mess up my purpose?'

After understanding your mission, come to understand the following: Who is my enemy? That is the "E" in METT-T. How did this person become my enemy? When did they become my enemy? What do we disagree on? The reason why you and the enemy are enemies is because he no longer has anointing. No wonder the moment you get even just a drop of anointing is when all hell breaks loose. The enemy is jealous of you. That is why when you find people in your space who are jealous of you you know they are demonic because anybody who has got anointing is not jealous of anybody else. The devil had no problem when you first got anointed, but when you started asking for more then there was a problem. I want more anointing! I need the kind of anointing that if a member of my family is sick, I can lay hands on them and they recover. I need an anointing where I can speak to any empty bank account and God gives me increase. I want the kind of anointing that causes demons to know me by name. That certainly gets the enemy up in arms against you.

You've got to know your mission, you've got to know who your enemy is, and then you've got to know what troops are available. The first "T" in METT-T is for troops. The attack is so intense and you've got to find out who can fight with you. The second "T" is for terrain. Not only do you have to be zealous, but you've got to have somebody who is trained for the environment you are about to go into. You've got to be connected to somebody else who has been through the same situation you have been. People who have been through nothing will be judgmental. Assess the troops that are fighting with you, find out if they've got experience in the terrain, and check their morale. If they get homesick easily then they are not the ones. You need to be positioned with people who will not leave until the battle is over. You need to get desperate people and not those who will keep looking at their watches in church, but rather those who will refuse to leave until the things that have been bothering them are dealt with.

The last "T" in METT-T is that you've got to give yourself a time limit. How much time are you going to spend fighting?

"I am not going to do this fighting all year. Lord, by Easter Sunday morning, I want this battle over." I am only fighting so that I can get to my place of victory; I am fighting so I can finally get peace in my house so that my children will be alright.

You have to move from being a soldier to becoming a guerilla fighter. In doing this, you start to do to the enemy what the enemy has been doing to you. So before he can go around talking about me, I am going ahead of him talking to people about me. I will tell them what I used to do and where I used to go and where I used to be. I will not be ashamed because if it had not been for the Lord, I would still be there. You cannot be a guerilla unless you go into his territory. You are not regular, but you are anointed and you are aspiring toward supernatural success.

> *You have to move from being a soldier to becoming a guerilla fighter. In doing this, you start to do to the enemy what the enemy has been doing to you.*

This is the season of your life where you have to almost act like a terrorist and do anything possible to win back your true self. Guerillas fight to get back the territory they lost. Whatever area of yourself you have lost, develop the attitude of guerilla warfare to get it back. Fight to be happy again, trust again, dream again, and for the right to be yourself again!

Chapter 16

COUNTERINTELLIGENCE

★

The enemy cannot control God's plan for your life because he has limited intelligence.

Jamal H. Bryant

I remember a time when our church was getting ready to make a long-awaited pivotal move. We had already moved from the nightclub we used, to a university and then to a high school. Finally, we had found our own sanctuary where we would be able to house two thousand five hundred people. Incidentally, the place we found to be our sanctuary was the very place where I had learned to roller skate. We had done everything we needed to do in terms of finances, organizational structure, and contracts, and we were now at the final threshold to our newfound home. Across the street from where our church is presently located is one of the city's oldest catering halls, owned by a minority business owner. It was strange that when we went to the authorities at City Hall for zoning, this African-American establishment followed us.

I was excited because I thought naively they had come to offer us support and to encourage our success, but much to my chagrin, these people came in and said we were going to be a threat to their business. Their establishment was not even a restaurant but rather a catering hall that was at the verge of collapse with minimal business to say the least. They came and asked City Hall authorities not to give us the permit we needed, claiming we would obstruct their business. I was hurt, wounded, and finally upset. The question ringing in my mind was how I could fight one of the guards of the city, one of the founding fathers, the sage of the community. I made up my mind to fight fire with fire.

That Sunday I went to our church and announced to everybody that the stumbling block to our progress was not racism, the government, or finance, but somebody who was in outright conflict with what we wanted to do. I then asked every member with a wedding reception, a high school reunion, or a bridal party to cancel all events scheduled for that establishment. I even asked them to influence every person they knew who had any dealings with that establishment. Sooner than later, the whole city was abuzz. Radio stations were calling, stories were featured in local newspapers, and even the family of the owner was calling me crying about how could I do this to their business. It was not something I had to do, but I understood that my ministry was on the line, the building was on the line, so I had to operate in a mode that I ordinarily wouldn't. Soon afterward, there was a sudden one hundred eighty degree shift. It was a risk for me to have done what I did and many said I was splitting my community, many others said I was anti- business, but I understood that I was in warfare, and because I was in warfare, I had to do everything I could do in order for the church to get to the next level. Do I have any regrets? Absolutely not! Because I had to take a hit, they had to take a boom.

Finally, we are in a place where both of us work in cohesion. Now after warfare is over, everybody understands the laws of war. Now we are in an amicable relationship, and we use their facility for youth church or overflow for special events, and the two of our entities now share parking space. I wonder what would have happened had

Many people miss their golden opportunity because they refuse to fight. Do not ever be afraid, ashamed, or intimidated.

I not taken the level of warfare I did. If I had bowed down and said I was not going to fight, I would not be where I am. Many people miss their golden opportunity because they refuse to fight. Do not ever be afraid, ashamed, or intimidated. When war comes to you, you cannot do otherwise. You have no choice but to stand up and swing forward.

In relation to the Vietnam War, President John F. Kennedy in 1962 said, 'This is another type of war. The intensity is as ancient as its origin. It is a war by outlaws and assassins; war by ambush instead of by combat. It is a war by infiltration instead of aggression; seeking victory by exhausting and eroding the enemy, instead of engaging him. We need a new kind of strategy, a different kind of force and a completely different kind of training because for this kind of battle we need a different kind of soldier."

What you are dealing with in your life is something that your parents may never have had to contend with. It is absolutely foreign terrain from what your grandparents had to fight and wrestle through. God is calling us to a unique kind of training, to an uncommon kind of force, and a different special strategy because the enemy is now fighting a different type of battle that is designed to be so intense that it might drain you to the point of quitting. We cannot fight the same way we used to fight because the enemy is now fighting with tactics that have not been approved. He is fighting in a way that is immoral, unethical, and goes against the grain of our call and our purpose. It would have been one thing if he had just fought us at the job and at home, but now he is fighting us over spiritual things. He now wants to take our focus off God, church, and our worship.

> *What you are dealing with in your life is something that your parents may never have had to contend with.*

The US Army in issuing out its manual in dealing with counterintelligence says, "In order for you to fight the enemy effectively you have to do three things. The first thing is that your fighting has got to be appropriate. Your level of fighting has got to be commensurate with your level of threat. If your threat is not so great then your fight does not have to be that great." Beloved, do not, from an outside perspective, judge the level of other people's worship without fully understanding the circumstances behind their praise.

For you it may be enough to simply wave your hand because you are not going though as much. But there is somebody that is worshiping God with a remarkable level of intensity because the level of attack on their life has been intense. If you are going through a battle you do not need anybody to beg you to worship God. When you are going through an attack on every side of your life, you do not even need an excuse, you do not need a drum or background music. All you have to think about is all of the struggles you've faced through this week and resolve in your mind that you will not carry the same weights throughout to the next week.

Second on the checklist, you have to make sure your fight is justifiable. If you cannot articulate the reason you are going to the battle, then it's not your battle. But when you understand there is purpose in your life, when you understand that there is a destiny and a goal you have not achieved yet and that the enemy is responsible for your difficulty in achieving them, then you can rise to the occasion and fight the enemy without hesitation or remorse. This is why you should not be connected to anybody who feels they have arrived. They have got nothing more to fight for. Get connected to somebody who is as hungry as you are and who wants to realize their dream as much as you do. When the people around you who lack vision, see you aspiring for greatness, they will argue that you're doing too much and will try throwing ice on the heat of your passion. But when you get to a point where you don't want to repeat the mistakes of your predecessors and you want to go farther than anybody in your family line, then you are anointed to do what others dared not do, and in so doing, you rewrite the legacy that has been branded into your family. You are bound to find yourself doing some things that nobody in your family line has ever been able to accomplish. The enemy knows you have the ability to singlehandedly disrupt a generational curse, so he wants to drag you back to the same cyrcle of mediocrity that other people related to you may have succumbed to. You have got to fight because you've got to break the generational curse. If you make it, everybody who comes behind you will operate under the same level of greatness you have pioneered.

The third thing you have to do is to find out how to use minimum force. You do not want to use all your energy in fighting, so you don't even have any energy left to celebrate the victory. There are people who are doing well, but cannot enjoy what they've got. They've finally got what they've been fighting for their whole life, but now after they have attained it they don't have energy enough to enjoy it. Make sure you reserve your strength. Don't go on expending all your energy on people who have no vision because when you realize your dream top they will not be there. Stop tracking down rumors because everybody that is talking about you does not have a life of their own. Please, stop staying up at night trying to figure out why people don't like you. After all, God did not call you out to be popular. He called you out to be effective. In essence, use minimum force for maximum benefit. You might have lost other things but you have not lost the bigger picture. Whatever setbacks you have experienced, they did not knock you out. Solomon says a righteous man falls seven times but rises again (Proverbs 24:16, 29:18). Similarly, every time the enemy knocks you down, wipe the blood from your lip and get up. You have the strength to bounce back up.

When you are engaged in counter-intelligence, you do not have advance warning. You've got to be ready at any moment to go into a fight. The enemy does not negotiate the terms. He comes when you least expect it. That's why you have to pray even when there is nothing wrong. You've got to worship even when it is not your fight. When you see somebody going

> ★
>
> *The enemy does not negotiate the terms. He comes when you least expect it. That's why you have to pray even when there is nothing wrong.*
>
> ★

through struggles, don't you dare try talking about them because the enemy is coming after you next. When you see somebody else going through a storm, start praying for them so that when you find yourself going through a storm somebody will be praying for you. You have to be ready at one moment's notice. The things you think are secure could be in the greatest peril.

Our grandparents were able to stay at a job for forty years and then get a gold watch. Here you are, probably thirty-four years old on your fifth job because there is nothing stable. The person you thought you were going to spend the rest of your life with, turns out to be more trouble in your camp. But God says that even though things around you have changed, *I am the same yesterday, today, and forever* (Hebrews 13:8). Friends may come, friends may go; you may have money for a fleeting moment before it slips through your fingers; jobs are awarded, come others are taken away; love may come and love may go, but God is here and He will never leave you. You are in training for the fight. Every time the Lord wakes you up in the morning, He is training you for what you do not have right now. When you go through storms, don't be discouraged; just get yourself ready because God is preparing to dispatch you for your assignment. Don't throw in the towel. Everything you have been through in your life was to prepare you for this moment.

Training is the cornerstone for success. You do not get to success without training for it. God wants to see whether you will still speak to people who you know don't like you. Will you bless those that don't like you? Will you support those who do not support your dream? Everything negative you go through in your life is training you for a greater good. If you cannot handle failure, how are you going to handle success? People are talking about you now when you don't have anything, so what do you think is going to happen when God finally opens the doors to your dream blessing?

You've got to fight with a purpose and with a resolution. Any man who has a relationship with a woman approaches a conversation different than a woman. When a man hears grievances and issues, he wants them resolved. He is asking, "What do I have to do?" The woman more often is not looking for immediate resolve rather for assessment. "I want to know why you did this," "Tell me what you were thinking." In some of the battles you go through, you do not have to make an assessment. Sometimes you just need to have a resolve. It must be over today. This is for those who have been in the fight of their lives and are tired of fighting and just want it over with.

In order to operate in counterintelligence and to expedite your impact, you need initiative, depth, and agility. Initiative gives you an edge over your enemy. You cannot wait to react. You have to predict his next move and then strike before he makes it. Don't wait for the enemy to attack because you know he will anyway. Your destiny is so great in your life that the enemy is going to do all he can to block you, so don't wait till the battle starts, start it. Start it in prayer, worship, and praise upfront.

Second, you need to know what the concept of depth is about. Get to know what your resources are and how far you are from them. You have to know your goal and what you are trying to achieve in life and how far you are from achieving it. The enemy does not launch an intense attack when you are still far; but rather when he sees you are getting close and you are just a few feet away from your target. That is when the attack is intensified. Be ready because the enemy is not going to fight with approved weapons. He will use weapons you have never seen or are not familiar with. The enemy always finds a covert agent. He will stick somebody in your camp that will get all the information and then turn that information against you, but you do not have to be overanxious about them because God is getting ready to expose the phony friends—people who are trying to get close to you only to know what you are up to and then derail it.

The enemy wants to delay, disrupt, and destroy. He wants to delay you from getting to your destiny. He wants to disrupt your focus and destroy your sense of self-identity. He comes to steal, kill, and destroy. Whenever there is a disruption in your life, know it is the enemy. He wants to disrupt you so that he can annoy and frustrate you. Don't allow anything to get in the way of your worship to God. In fact, the more irritated you are, the more intense your worship should be.

After your disruption, how do you handle delay? Are you confusing delay with denial? You may have thought you would be far by now and some things would be in place, but things seem to drag. Well, find solace in the scripture that says, *The race is not given to the swift, nor to the strong, but to the one who waits* (Ecclesiastes 9:11, paraphrased).

The enemy can destroy you if he convinces you that what you believe God for is not going to happen. He can destroy you emotionally more than the atomic bomb can do to you physically. You have to safeguard your mind in the face of delays and in the face of distractions. You have to tell yourself over and over that what you believe God for is still going to happen. No matter what it looks like right now, it's still going to happen.

The third thing that will enable you to operate in counterintelligence is agility, which is the power to handle a situation even when that situation changes suddenly. Paul learned how to be abased and how to abound· He learned how to live in the overflow and how to live in lack, and no matter what state he was in, he still knew how to trust God. The enemy does not know what to do with you because your life keeps changing from strength to strength.

★

The enemy can destroy you if he convinces you that what you believe God for is not going to happen.

★

In being trained for this kind of warfare, you have to learn to fight with limited logistics. First you are fighting in a territory with which you are not familiar, and you don't even know when backup is coming and you don't even know how long your resources are going to last, but you fight anyway with undiminished resolve. It takes a person of faith to fight even when they do not know where they are going. You don't have many bullets left. You cannot waste bullets on moving objects. You've got to zero in on the threat.

If there was one thing you could wipe out today, what would it be? If you can get rid of the biggest thing, these other little things will not be much of a problem. It is God's full intention for you to destroy the biggest demon in your life. That's why He gives the reassurance that *no weapon formed against you will prosper* (Isaiah 54:17, paraphrased).

The fight you are up against is because the enemy is trying to drain your strength. He wants to make you weak and dilapidated so the next time he attacks, you won't even have the strength to fight. You've got to reserve your strength for the next hit. You need to refuel and get into the best shape of your life. Fight like you have never fought in your life. The enemy is after your strength. He wants to deplete you of any resources and artillery you have left. He wants you to get so worn out from fighting that you lose your sense of agility and perseverance. Be encouraged though. The enemy can't halt God's plan for your life. He doesn't know that God is capable of reversing his intent. The devil thought he was going to burn you out from delay, but he did not know what was happening to you in the middle of the delay. The enemy cannot control God's plan for your life because he has limited intelligence.

> ★
>
> *The enemy cannot control God's plan for your life because he has limited intelligence.*
>
> ★

Chapter 17

ASSIGNED FOR
SPECIAL FORCES

★

Whenever the enemy captures someone out of special training, they will take more time to torture them because there is more investment in them.

Jamal H. Bryant

On July 6, 1916, for the very first, time a poster was released in the *Lesley Weekly* that would soon become the most famous poster in the entire world. The poster read, WE WANT YOU FOR UNCLE SAM'S ARMY. Between 1917 and 1918, four million copies of this poster were distributed. According to the Library of Congress, that picture of Uncle Sam is the most known picture that represents the United States of America. The posters were designed to increase and to instill patriotism, enlarge recruitment efforts, provoke conservation and productivity and investment. Ironically, in modern times it would appear the poster is about recruitment of people yet the original intent of the poster was not to get people but to get the resources people had.

In the heat of the battle you have to understand that the enemy really is not impressed by who you really are on the outside, but rather the spiritual nature that is sustaining you on the inside. In the heat of the battle the enemy wants to capture elite soldiers or Special Forces.

> ★
>
> *If you have been going through a targeted attack, it's a sign that the enemy knows how special you are.*
>
> ★

The military invests more money on Special Forces because they hold more secrets. They have in their minds patterns, diagrams, charts, and exit and entry strategies that regular soldiers would not have access to. Whenever the enemy captures someone out of the elite source or has special training, they will take more time to torture them because there is more investment in them.

If you have been going through a targeted attack, it's a sign that the enemy knows how special you are. You are not regular because you know some secrets that other people don't know. You know how to get in and how to get out of situations without ever being scarred or burned. God knows

He has made a major investment in you since He had to get you out of more stuff than He has regular people. The enemy knows if he can get you then he would have made a tremendous feat. You are special to God. You are not regular, you are not ordinary, you are not mundane but you are special. You are so special to Him that two thousand years ago before you were even born He went on a hill called Calvary and said, "I will die for you" in advance. You were never designed to be like everybody else. You were never created to fit in the crowd, but you are fearfully and wonderfully made. You are so special that no matter where you are, you never fit in the status quo because God has made you special. No wonder everybody wanted to get to Jesus. He walked into sermons and disrupted worship. He preached sermons without ever being ordained, testifying in the marketplace. He performed miracles to people who were the least, the lost, and the leftover. No wonder they wanted Jesus dead because He knew who He was and cared less what people said about Him. The enemy wants you dead because you've got healthy self-esteem. You are not arrogant but convinced that you are anointed from the top of your head down to the soles of your feet. The enemy wants you dead because you disrupt worship and you won't wait for a convenient time to thank God. He wants you dead because you are a breathing, living, walking miracle.

It would have been enough to crucify Him but because they understood that Jesus was the most elite special force, they had to put Him in a tomb. The tomb is in fact illegal detainment. When there is a call on your life and a purpose on your destiny, with a special anointing on your promise then the enemy will try to put you into detainment, which is when you feel like you are not making any progress, like you are stuck in a situation and can't move forward and can't move back. Detainment is when your movement is controlled. Then you have some people in your life who are Centurion soldiers, trying to keep you in one place and in one position. When they see you begin to make progress, they try to stop you and block you.

The enemy wants to detain you. It is the diabolic scheme of the captor to make you overwhelmed with loneliness and boredom. When you are assigned with purpose, the enemy will try to make you feel like you are in it by yourself. The enemy knows there is strength in numbers, especially when you are in the fellowship of believers. He wants you isolated and lonely and also drives you to the place where you are bored and unmotivated. He wants you to run out of gas, and though you know there is a purpose on you, you just don't feel like it anymore.

When the enemy has you captive, he will torture you. In Vietnam in 1969, there was something called the Hanoi Hilton, which was a metaphor for a torture cage. When the captors had one of the US soldiers in prison, they would torture the captive until everybody else in the cell was able to hear what was going on. They hoped that when they heard the scream of somebody who was being tortured they would release information. But in Vietnam training they were told in order for you to get through that kind of psychological trauma, when you hear somebody in your cell screaming, don't sit there because it will eat up your mind, but when they start screaming, scream with them so that the person who is going through torture will know that somebody else feels their pain. The second reason why they would scream was to let the captor know that what you are doing to my friend, he is not in it by himself, but I am going through it with him. The enemy wants to torture you by intimidating the people close to you. They will do everything they can to break your will to live. You have to make up in your mind that no matter what you go through, your spirit will not be broken. Your bank account may be depleted, your family may be a broken home, but your spirit should never break.

> *The enemy wants to torture you by intimidating the people close to you.*

When you find your self in a tomb situation, there are four things you have to do: The first thing is control what can be controlled. In other words, when you are stuck, remind yourself who you are and what you are trained to do. You have to start talking to yourself. When failures start popping up, talk to yourself: "This is my year of supernatural success. Failure is not an option, and mediocrity is not a choice. Weeping may endure for the night but joy comes in the morning. He may not come when I want him but He is right on time."

Second, keep your mind alert. Start writing a novel in your own mind. The novel is not based on where you are but where you want to be. Create a series in your mind, a reality show, and God is getting ready to turn what you have in your mind into reality. Have the business in your mind, have that marriage in your mind. See your children doing better. See yourself as the head and not the tail.

Third, when you are stuck in a tomb experience, plan your escape. Even if it looks impossible, an opportunity is going to come where you are going to be able to run for it. Today might be your opportunity to run for it and nobody will stop you.

> *If Jesus Christ can get up and walk out of the tomb, you and I can escape and conquer anything.*

When you plan your escape you have to have an idea of where you want to go. Don't plan your escape if you don't know where you want to go. If you have no purpose, you might as well sit and cross your legs. You have to know that when you escape there has to be some distance between where you are and where you are going. When God gets you out of this, you are never going back to where you used to be. Are you ready for a fresh start and a fresh beginning? You will never be broke like that, never be frustrated like that, and never be sad like that again. I've got too much to live for to die right now. God promised me too much.

Jesus is in the tomb by Himself, and He knows where He is going. I grew up AME and I'm still AME, and in order for us to graduate we had to learn the Apostles creed: I believe in God the Father, maker of the heaven and the earth, Jesus Christ our Lord and savior; born of a virgin Mary; suffered under Pontius Pilate; was crucified, died, and was buried; descended into hell; then on the third day he ascended into heaven." After Jesus went through His crucifixion, to His tomb, the first place He went to was hell. Some people don't understand that you are one step away from your destiny because you have been living in hell all this time, but God says this is just one stop before I get you to your purpose. The only reason you went to hell was to get some people out. When you get out you are taking your family with you. What good would the resurrection be if He just got up and out for Himself? The beauty of resurrection is that when Jesus got out, He took all of us with Him. Today you are getting out of some stuff, and not just you but everyone connected to you.

I am unashamed to admit I am a devout fan of all the James Bond movies. I love how in every seemingly impossible situation, he survives. The author, Ian Fleming, has a vivid imagination with which he creates the most peculiar things to assist Agent 007's escape. The truth is, it is all a hoax—a fake. The upside of Fleming's fiction is the fact it creates greater respect and reverence for the greatest miracle of all: the resurrection of Jesus, which is completely real. Think on this: If Jesus Christ can get up and walk out of the tomb, you and I can escape and conquer anything.

Chapter 18

DESERT STORM

If you're going through hell
Keep on going, don't slow down.
If you're scared, don't show it.
You might get out before the devil even knows
you're there.
If You're Going Through Hell

Rodney Atkins

W hen we applied for a zoning permit to operate our church at the new location, the owner of the catering business across the street opposed us. As a result, the city denied our request. That was one of the darkest seasons of my life. I had a difficult time dealing with that denial. To me, it was inexplicable. We had already closed on the purchase, obligated ourselves on a mortgage, and begun construction. The congregation was mobilized and energized for the move, then the city turned us down.

In the weeks following the city's decision, I slipped into a season of depression. I didn't want to sleep, eat, or drink. Doubt followed close behind. I started thinking maybe I wasn't practicing what I preached. I always had tried to instill in our members that faith is the only thing that will sustain you when life is trying to break you. Now, I was breaking and crying and questioning God, asking Him why He was doing all this to us—to me. We'd been on a journey since that first service in the nightclub and were about to step into the Promised Land. Then, on the brink of crossing over into greatness, the door was slammed in our face.

Slowly, I began to hear God's voice. He said to me, "How do you think the children of Israel felt when they had to walk through the wilderness and couldn't get into the Promised Land? Did they stop or did they keep marching?" I had to keep on marching.

Not long after that, my former wife challenged me. She looked me straight in the eye and said, "How do you call yourself a pastor? This is the season when you have to preach to yourself. The same thing that you tell your congregation is what you have to tell yourself now. He may not come when you want Him to come, but He is an on-time God."

I started getting up early every morning and began writing the script for the dedication ceremony. Sometimes, I would wake up in the middle of the night and write out how we would conduct our inaugural service. In the heat of the afternoon, I would stop what I was doing and start imagining what the balcony was going to look like, what the dancers would look like, and what the color lines around the building would be.

Sure enough, because we kept marching and pushing, God kept us strong. We did not give up. We kept going down to City Hall to meet with the city council officials. I didn't stop until I met the mayor himself. We were relentless because we understood we were in a dry season, in the middle of a drought with nothing growing and with no affirmative answers. Over time, I came to feel in my heart what I spoke with my lips, that this was a season that would pass like all others.

The city councilman designated for our area told our team he was against the move. His argument was that our church was going to cause a traffic problem. The traffic flow in the community would be disrupted, but we weren't going to give up, not after coming this far. We kept moving. The vice president of the city council also was against our plan. He suggested we look for another option. He said what we were trying to do would never happen.

We kept pressing forward. Fellow preachers started calling me, saying, "Maybe this isn't going to happen for you. Maybe you misunderstood God. Maybe you heard wrong," but we kept pressing forward through that dry, desertlike season.

When people in authority and positions of influence don't believe in your dream, when they try to suck up and dry your faith, you're in a desert. I was reminded of the words of David in 1 Samuel 30:6 while he was in the cave of Adullam, *I encouraged myself in the Lord.*

Every Sunday while we were meeting in the high school auditorium, I would tell the congregation we only had a few weeks before we entered our new building. This was the same building from which the city council was trying to block us. The same building that high-ranking politicians didn't believe we could have. The same building that was blocked by all three administrative associations. The same building that caused preachers to mock me. The only thing that was sustaining us was the purpose God had for our lives. There comes a place in every believer's life where you have to live through a desert, where nothing is growing, moving, or developing around you. The only thing that will sustain you is your promise—that unique word God has given you about your destiny.

When the first crisis in the Persian Gulf hit in 1991, it was America's first major military operation since the Vietnam War. Many of the president's advisors were tremendously concerned whether the troops were prepared for the fight. The last time America had been engaged in a fight, they were in a thick jungle. The Persian Gulf was a wide open desert. The concern was whether we were equipped to fight in an environment we had never been in before. Would our artillery hold up? Would our machinery handle the change of climate?

A desert is a barren, desolate place. It's a place of extreme temperatures, fluctuating from bone-chilling cold at night to scorching heat during the day. Ecologically and geologically, it's a place where no growth occurs.

Even though you may not have been to a desert in the physical sense, we all have been through a spiritual desert storm at one time or another. A place in our lives where nothing manifested from our gift and nothing grew. A place with no support mechanism or resources. A place with nothing around us to equip us for survival or energize us for the next mile ahead. Sometimes when we get into a desert we are there at the Lord's direction, not the enemy's misdirection.

★

Even though you may not have been to a desert in the physical sense, we all have been through a spiritual desert storm at one time or another.

★

In Matthew 14:13–16 Jesus stepped off a ship and walked into a desert. He walked from a place saturated with water into a place saturated with dryness. When He walked into that desert, a small group accompanied Him. Jesus needed people who would be with Him in the season of abundance and people who would follow Him through the times of lack, when nothing was growing. In verse 14, Jesus found the same core that was with Him in the water also was with Him in the desert. He had compassion on them because they didn't just follow Him in the good times, but even when the environment didn't seem very promising and inviting. He then began to heal them right in the middle of a desert.

God doesn't need a perfect environment to bless us. He can bless us even when nothing is going right in our lives.

In verse 15, the religious people—the "church" people—came up to Jesus and advised him to send the crowd away because there was nothing for them to eat in the desert. Jesus refused. Instead, he insisted that they stay and then made sure their needs were met right there in the desert.

> *God doesn't need a perfect environment to bless us. He can bless us even when nothing is going right in our lives.*

God is with you when you are in the wilderness. Your needs are still going to be met. In the presence of God, even when nothing seems to be working for you, you can find comfort in the knowledge that He will not abandon you to the harshness of the environment. He is God even in the middle of a desert.

In a desert you are forced to live with limited resources. In order to survive you have to adapt to the situation. God might not have blessed you with overflow, but He is your all-sufficiency. You might not have very much, but you have enough to make it. It might not be what you want, but it will be what you need. The gas is still running, the car has not been repossessed, the children are healthy and happy.

Sometimes God lets you go through a desert situation so you can see how hard you will fight for what you know is your rightful destiny. Are you willing to make it even when all you have are bare necessities? God has not promised that you will always have whatever you want whenever you want it. He has promised you daily bread. So keep moving in the direction of your dream no matter what the terrain. The key to success is the resolve to keep moving even when you are drained—the ability to hang on. The soldiers God is recruiting to fight in the desert are those who have learned to make it off a little bit, those who have learned to live without, who press forward even when they are exhausted.

There are three kinds of deserts. The first is the mountain desert—high, dry places. These are the people who, by outward appearances, have attained a high level of success, yet inside, they are miserable. A person can be in a high place and still be unfilled, unhappy, and dissatisfied.

The second kind of desert is a rocky plateau. Flat and featureless for a distance, it drops into a canyon, then rises back up to a peak. These are the people whose lives are in a period of inconsistency. People you could count on yesterday are gone today. God doesn't want you to rely on consistency in other people but to look for it in Him. He never changes. He's the same yesterday, today, and forever.

The third kind of desert is the sandy one. Nothing grows there—no vegetation, no water, no reservoir for nutrients. This is that time in your life when you have been anointed for greatness, but you find yourself surrounded by nothing. People around you can't understand why you have so much life, yet there is no life in those around you. To survive in that environment, you have to grow as a plant with no attention or cultivation. You have to be your own mentor and own example. Your own leader. Everyone wants to be connected to a success, but not many want to be associated with someone who is struggling, trying to find their way in the dark.

These three kinds of deserts have one thing in common. They all are places without much life. From all outward appearances, they are dead places. Whether you have a Ph.D. or a G.E.D., there are things in your life that are dead— things that need cultivation and development, things that need to be pulled up and thrown away. Those are the areas that God is going to press you to fight through. Not the area you show everyone and talk about, but the area that is dead. God is finally going to cause you to deal with the area that embarrasses you. This may sound like bad news, but here is the good part: God will never get you into a fight without giving you sufficient strength and backup to win it. Facing those dead spots in your life is essential to your continued growth and the full manifestation of your gift. To reach your destiny, you must face those dead spots, those dry and barren areas of your life.

In order for you to be successful in a desert, you have to be able to run a long way without the need for refueling. A camel is a great desert animal because it can go a month without being fed. It can go two weeks without getting water. With no food and water, the average camel can carry four hundred pounds.

Some of you have been carrying a lot of weight without much relief. People around you have no idea how much you've handled and how long you've been handling it. You just kept pushing forward, one foot in front of the other. Now that you look back, you can't even remember how you got this far. That's life in a desert—one step at a time.

From this day forward, purpose in your heart to stop comparing your life to someone else's. You have no idea how much weight they are carrying. Things may not be as rosy as they seem in that other person's life. Rather than looking at them with envy, get to know them. You might learn something that will help you, and you might be a blessing in the midst of a misery you never knew existed.

From this day forward, purpose in your heart to stop comparing your life to someone else's. You have no idea how much weight they are carrying.

In war, the best troops get sent to the worst places. If you are in a desert place, you were drafted because God knew you would not break in that environment. Just keep moving. You are in the desert for a season. You won't be there forever. This is not the end. Where you are is not where you are supposed to stay. Keep moving!

While you are in the desert, you are going to run into desert dwellers—people who have made the desert their home. Don't give in to the temptation to join them. You're a traveler. You live in a tent. You're only there temporarily. The desert dwellers are the ones who gave up and built a house rather than fight through to the other side. They built a house in the midst of their misery, one with small windows because they have no vision. Those who are anointed have large windows in their spirits through which they look with the perspective of God. He continually expands visions for their life. Be careful. When you start seeing small you know you have been adopted by the desert. You are in danger of becoming a desert dweller.

One of the most priceless assets in a desert is water. You have to safeguard your water in the desert. The supply you need is not on the surface. You have to dig deeper. This is that time in your life when you have to look to the Holy Spirit like never before. Jesus said in John 7:37–38, *"If anyone is thirsty, let him come to me and drink. Whoever believes in me, as the Scripture has said, streams of living water will flow from within him."* When you are in a spiritual desert, your life is in a crucial place. You are there to learn deeper things of God, things you need for the rest of your journey, and things you can't learn any other way.

After an extended period in the desert, some people report seeing mirages. Heat and distance combine to bend the intense light to create optical illusions. Images appear in front of you, which your mind twists to look like whatever it is you might think you need or want. The shimmering heat becomes a pool of water. You jump into it to find it is only sand. A rock in the distance becomes a truck. You run toward it to find out there is nothing there but the rock.

When you've gone a long distance in a spiritual desert, you start to look for the one thing that is going to extract you from your circumstances—the one "magic solution" to your situation. There might be a solution like that just up ahead, but most of the time getting through the desert comes by putting one foot in front of the other. Just keep moving. Don't get caught up in chasing the magic solution. God is your answer. He will guide you to the next oasis, and then across the desert to fertile ground.

The last thing you need to know about fighting in the desert storm is acclimation. For the average American soldier, getting used to a new environment requires roughly two weeks of exposure to it. The Lord doesn't want you to get used to the spiritual desert—at least not like the desert dwellers—but He certainly wants you to adjust to it. Adjust to the situation you are in, but make up your mind never to get comfortable with it. You'll find this means adjusting your attitude. If you ignored self-discipline before, you'll quickly find it essential to survive in the desert. If you avoided self-control, you'll learn that in the desert too. Adjust. Adapt. But don't give in.

Crossing the desert is a long, hot trek. Along the way, you get rid of a lot of the junk you've been carrying around. I'm sure the wagon trails westward were littered with all the extra things settlers started with, things they were sure they couldn't live without: pianos, stacks of dishes, party dresses, and pump organs. Packing that stuff across a desert forces you to throw out everything except the essentials: food, water, clothing, weapons for hunting and protection, and tools for building a house when you reach your destination. Most everything else gets thrown away and left behind. That's the kind of spiritual journey you will encounter in the desert. You go in packing a lot of weight on your back. You come out stripped down, lean, agile, and far stronger than when you first began.

Chapter 19

D-DAY

---★---

Finally, be strong in the Lord and in his mighty power. Put on the full armor of God so that you can take your stand against the devil's schemes. For our struggle is not against flesh and blood, but against the rulers, against the authorities, against the powers of this dark world and against the spiritual forces of evil in the heavenly realms. Therefore put on the full armor of God, so that when the day of evil comes, you may be able to stand your ground, and after you have done everything, to stand. Stand firm then, with the belt of truth buckled around your waist, with the breastplate of righteousness in place, and with your feet fitted with the readiness that comes from the gospel of peace.

—Ephesians 6:10-15

On the morning of June 6, 1944, more than eleven thousand airplanes flew sorties over France. Five thousand ships lay off the coast of Normandy. Scattered somewhere between those ships and the beach were one hundred fifty thousand soldiers. They had been on those ships for weeks, waiting for the order to move out. By then, many of them were seasick. They knew the German army awaited them on the beach, and they knew a withering barrage of gunfire would be coming at them from every angle, but for some, being on those ships was more than they could bear. They'd trained hard for the coming mission. They'd been looking to this day for a long time. Training was over. D-Day had arrived. It was time to go.

The prophet Joel spoke of a similar day. He didn't call it D-Day. He called it, "The day of the Lord." He saw that day as actually three days. A day of the Lord in the past when God revealed Himself to Israel and called them into relationship with Him, a day of the Lord in the present, where He is active in current events, and a day of the Lord in the future when God will move in human history in a dramatic fashion.

Whether that day is in the past, present, or future, it has two aspects. It is a time when the Lord gives Himself to us as never before.

I will pour out my Spirit on
all people.
Your sons and daughters will
prophesy,
your old men will dream
dreams,

230

your young men will see
visions.

—Joel 2:28

And it is a time of judgment.
The sun will be turned to
darkness
and the moon to blood
before the coming of the
great and dreadful day of
the Lord.

—Joel 2:31

Paul picked up this theme in some of his writings. His most poignant reference comes at the end of his letter to the church at Ephesus. Most of that epistle deals with the accomplishments of Christ and the transforming nature of a relationship with Him. In fact, Paul spends six chapters on that topic. Then, in the latter half of the last chapter he turns to the subject of a coming day.

Paul used that half chapter to talk about how the believer's life of transformation is really a life of warfare. By positioning it near the end, following a lengthy discussion of the effect Christ has on the life of a believer, Paul emphasized the notion that attack from the enemy occurs most noticeably after you have entered that transforming process. To be sure, all who are without a saving relationship with Jesus are being deceived, but the most savage attack on a believer comes after the point of commitment.

To face that coming battle, Paul describes the armor available and encourages believers to avail themselves of every piece. Many of us can recite the verses from Ephesians 6:14–17, listing the individual pieces and their uses. But Paul is not simply giving an equipment checklist. A checklist alone is only a checklist. It only tells you what to wear. It doesn't tell you what to do. Soldiers need orders. Someone has to tell them when to march and which direction to go. Paul provides those orders in verse 13: *"Therefore put on the full armor of God, so that when the day of evil comes, you may be able to stand your ground, and after you have done everything, to stand."*

Suit up. Put on the armor. A day of evil is coming.

Everything you have gone through already has trained you for one specific day. That day is today. That day is also tomorrow. We aren't promised tomorrow and are prohibited from knowing what will happen in the future, except as God reveals it, but you can be sure, everything you went through in your past was preparation for the divine moment of the present. And everything you experience today will prepare you for tomorrow—the present of tomorrow.

Paul uses the term *evil day* because it speaks of a particular day and a particular time. Every day is not the same. There is an evil day historically when the apocalyptic end appears. There have been evil days in your past when all hell broke loose on you and destruction seemed to reign, and there is an evil day in your present circumstances when the enemy thinks it's a day on which you are most vulnerable. Satan is looking for the day when you are at your weakest—a day when you aren't paying attention. He lurks in the corner, hidden by the folds in the drapery, peering out from the shadows and asking, "Is this the day I can break you?"

Many of you aren't fighting against an evil day. You're fighting to find just one good day—one day when nothing goes wrong, when you don't have to deal with trauma, when you can sleep through the whole night. You aren't looking for an extended season. Just one good day is all you're asking for. Those days come too.

When that evil day comes, you don't know how the enemy is going to attack or from which direction he will arrive. Rest assured, when the attack comes it won't be from just one direction. He will come at you from every available angle.

Jack Hayford, pastor of Church on the Way, wrote a book a few years ago called *How To Handle A Bad Day.* In that book he talked about what Jesus went through on the cross—a day when He forgave people who didn't even recognize the greatness in Him. A day when He had to take care of His family even though His family didn't take care of Him. A day when He had to forgive people seated right beside Him as friends who also betrayed Him. You will have those days too.

Some of you are in really tough situations. Supplies you needed yesterday didn't arrive, and now you are on the brink of giving up on God today. God hasn't forgotten about you. There are people around you who were designated to help you. Some of them don't always pay attention. Both obedience and disobedience have an effect on those around us. When God lays something on your heart— take some money to this person—and you don't obey, that other person suffers the consequences. God always has a backup plan, but your lack of obedience delays the whole process and causes unnecessary grief. For the one on the brink, hang on. Help is on the way. For the one receiving the word from God, get moving. Time is of the essence.

The events of D-Day are a good example of what I'm talking about. The night before the attack, our bombers bombed the French coast in an effort to minimize resistance to our troops when they landed. Planes dropped paratroopers behind enemy lines to disrupt communications and to be ready when troops on the beach broke out. Everyone followed a well-crafted plan. Then reality hit.

Most of the planes with the paratroopers couldn't find their drop zones. Paratroopers landed in the wrong places and were scattered everywhere. Pilots flying the bombers couldn't find the drop zones either. Afraid they would bomb their own soldiers, they dropped their bombs too far inland to have any effect on the beach areas.

Ships carrying all those troops were eleven miles offshore. They were safely out of range of the German cannons on the shore, but so far out the landing craft had a tough time getting the troops to the beach. When they reached the beach, the men driving the boats zigged and zagged trying to dodge enemy gunfire. As a result, most of them were seriously off course.

By dawn, thousands of soldiers were struggling to get from the water to a low berm a few yards up the beach. No one was where he was supposed to be. Supplies were at the bottom of the ocean. Most of the tanks were there too.

That's when Plan A went out the window. What was supposed to happen didn't. Someone—many someones—failed to properly execute their assignments, so sergeants and lieutenants on the beach took charge. They rounded up the men nearest them, regardless of which company they were assigned to, and formed ad-hoc units. Weapons and explosives were scavenged from the beach. Slowly they worked their way up, blowing holes in the heavily mined German defenses and inching their way forward. Plan A wasn't executed correctly by the people to whom the tasks were assigned, yet the alternative plan improvised on the beach turned out to be even better than the original one.

Offshore, Naval commanders aboard the huge flotilla of ships saw what was happening and heard the reports of what went wrong. That's when their plans were tossed aside too. In violation of direct orders, and ignoring the threat of the German defenses, commanders steered their ships to within a thousand yards of shore. This dramatically cut the distance for the landing craft and gave the men a much better opportunity to reach the beach alive and intact. At the same time, the ships turned their huge cannons on the German positions. Soldiers reached the beach in better fighting shape, and cannon shells rained down on the German defenders. The new, improvised plan worked far better than the original one.

God has a Plan A for your life. He has a plan to elevate you from your present situation. If those around you don't cooperate with His purposes, then Plan A might get frustrated, but that's alright. God has a Plan B, and God's Plan B is just as good as, or better than His Plan A.

During World War II, Hitler and the German army attacked their neighboring countries. They also attacked an entire generation and a race of people. Their aim was to wipe that race from the earth. Today, this present generation faces an attack as well.

> *In Baltimore, fifty percent of all city school students will drop out by the eleventh grade.*

In Baltimore, fifty percent of all city school students will drop out by the eleventh grade. When you walk through the high schools in the city, you see girls who want to be boys and boys who want to be girls. Kids regularly abuse alcohol and drugs and they engage in promiscuous sexual activity in ways you don't want to know about. Much of what they're doing comes from a pattern of conduct they observe at home.

Parents, trying to cope with their problems, or perhaps just being self-centered, medicate themselves on Friday and Saturday night and spend the weekend in an intoxicated haze. Some even stagger into church that way on Sunday. They move from partner to partner in a dizzying round of unstable relationships that cater only to their physical desires.

Then everyone wonders why the fastest growing institution in the State of Maryland is the state penitentiary. Things are so bad the authorities are creating jails for children as young as the sixth grade.

Violence among African-Americans has killed more of us than the Ku Klux Klan ever did. Drugs are sold on the street corners of our communities and from the steps of our own apartment buildings. All the while our children are saying, "I want to be a hustler."

Someone sound the alarm! We are under attack.

> *Someone sound the alarm! We are under attack.*

There is a day coming for the church, but it won't be our D-Day. For the Kingdom of God, D-Day came some two thousand years ago on a hill called Calvary. When they put our Savior on the cross, the sun refused to shine, the flowers refused to bloom, the birds refused to sing. The earth was dark for three hours because all of Creation knew something was happening. Jesus stormed the gates of hell that day. He drove back the enemy, vanquished every foe, and set the captives free. He won the victory.

Our day is not a day of invasion. Our day is a day of standing, of refusing to run when Satan mounts his counterattacks against our victory. We stand in a position of strength. All we have to do is hold our ground.

When the day gets dark in your life, things can get ugly. Things can get hard. That doesn't mean God isn't working. In fact, those are the days He's doing the most for you. Often when things get darkest, God is shifting some powerful things in your life. Times get rough because Satan doesn't want you to have what God wants to give you.

The Day of the Lord is a day of judgment. It is also a day of blessing. God can work wonders in a day. He's already shown us what He can do. In a single day, He raised Jesus from the dead. In a single day, He parted the Red Sea. In a single day, He sent manna from heaven, fed thousands, healed the sick, and raised the dead.

Everything you need can be fixed by God in a single day. That wonderful Day of the Lord.

In one day, you can be delivered from old habits, from poverty, from people in your life who are holding you back. In one day you can walk away from cigarettes. In one day you can walk away from drug addiction. In one day you can tell your lesbian lover that you are through with that relationship. In one day you can get away from a homosexual lifestyle that has been eating you alive. Everything that is in your life and is not of God, you can give it an eviction notice right now. It will be gone in a single day.

Today is the Day of the Lord.

THE VETERANS HOSPITAL

★

"The church is the only army that gets rid of its wounded soldiers."

Anonymous

Recently, I heard an older preacher say, "The church is the only army that gets rid of its wounded soldiers." Regrettably, in far too many instances, that has proven to be true. I'll never forget an occasion I had to speak at the Veterans Hospital in the nation's capitol. It was one of the most startling and inspiring moments in my ministry. Along the corridors, I passed people with missing limbs, eye bandages, wheelchairs, crutches, breathing devices, and body casts. The realization that all of them were wounded in battle fighting for the freedom of others is absolutely humbling. Their names weren't in the paper, their pictures weren't on CNN, they wore no medals on their chests, but they had absolutely no shame, guilt, or embarrassment. They were proud of what they were a part of and considered their sacrifice a labor of love. Before I spoke, the chaplain whispered to me, "Don't feel sorry for them. They are soldiers! They may be wounded in body, but they are strong in spirit."

As I write this, I want you to know that I am a patient in the Veterans Hospital. God is still healing me as He is doing for many of you. You might not recognize me right now because I have on eye bandages due to my sin. I lost sight of my priorities which were my family and my ministry. Some days I've been in a wheelchair going to the pulpit because I didn't think I'd be able to stand, to speak on God's behalf, or face the thousands who I disappointed.

> ★
>
> *Folly is bound up in the hearts of all God's children, and the rod is necessary to rebuke, to subdue, and to humble.*
>
> ★

There are moments where I've hobbled along on crutches leaning on the wisdom of my mentors, the encouragements of my friends, and the prayers of my parents. Honestly, my limbs have all been intact but there were nights I woke up feeling like I had lost heart because depression was creeping in, anxiety was always around, and stress covered me like a blanket. The only thing that kept me alive was the breathing device of praise and worship. It was David that declared in Psalm 150:6, "*Let everything that has breath praise the Lord.*" Praise has sustained me when life has deflated me. Whatever you do, don't feel sorry for me. I am a soldier.

What I went through is not what the devil made me do. It was a lack of self-discipline, selfishness, and greed.

Folly is bound up in the hearts of all God's children, and the rod is necessary to rebuke, to subdue, and to humble. Divine chastisement is designed for our good, to promote our highest interests, and bring us nearer to God to make us more like Him.

You cannot chastise a wild vagrant child making noise on the streets. But if you, as a parent, were to see your child bringing chaos in the street or otherwise engaging in misconduct himself, you would chastise him because it's your child; you are interested enough in him not to let him act a fool. And therefore, while you pass the rest by, as having no concern in them, you bring your own child under special chastening. Spiritually, the wild vagrants to whom the Lord has no regard have no rod of chastisement; they are left to their own ways. But the heirs of promise, the children of the living God, cannot be allowed to go astray.

This is best echoed in Hebrews 12:7-11.

Endure hardship as discipline; God is treating you as sons. For what son is not disciplined by his father? If you are not disciplined (and everyone undergoes discipline), then you are illegitimate children and not true sons. Moreover, we have all had human fathers who disciplined us and we respected them for it. How much more should we submit to the Father of our spirits and live!

Our fathers disciplined us for a little while as they thought best; but God disciplines us for our good, that we may share in his holiness. No discipline seems pleasant at the time, but painful. Later on, however, it produces a harvest of righteousness and peace for those who have been trained by it. (NIV)

Throughout history, most wars are conducted alongside partners and allies. On one hand are allies you are fighting for—your family, friends, and fans who believe in you and your purpose. On the other hand are allies whose aim is to distract you by inciting you to participate in activities that you know will lead you to a battlefield for which you are ill-equipped. These allies invite you into a world that shrouds good judgment, weakens your borders, and makes you susceptible for attack. Choosing to fall into the temptation these types of allies offer may seem like an individual choice, but you soon realize the fate of both yourself and your loved ones is in your hands.

In the aftermath of any war, there are casualties. Some die on the battlefield, but many who survive become your POWs—your walking wounded whose injuries you could have prevented. In the case of my war, my family, friends, and parishioners became POWs afflicted by anger, bitterness, disillusionment, disappointment, and shame. I was a willing victim, but they were caught in the crossfire of my choices and were punished for their association with me. For those of you on the cusp of choosing to fight on a battlefield with allies, who don't have your best interest at heart, use my story as an example for which choices to avoid. Do what you can to protect your loved ones, to keep them from becoming your walking wounded, from making them causalities of your war.

It's my hope that my injuries will help you not just survive, but thrive as you come out of your own personal World War Me. I must warn you that when you endure like a good soldier, your name won't make it into the church bulletin, your picture won't be held up on Christian television, and no special plaques or corsages will be presented in your honor. However, you will be able to hear God say, "Well done!"

> ★
>
> *Do what you can to protect your loved ones, to keep them from becoming your walking wounded, from making them causalities of your war.*
>
> ★

Upon leaving the hospital, they took me another route and this time I passed by the rehabilitation center. The same patients I passed in the hall were now going through treatment—learning how to walk again, some with prosthetic attachments; some were practicing speech; some were being weaned off the devices so they could breathe independently; and others were getting their eyes checked. Two things you must know are:

1. All the patients were determined to make the hospital temporary.

2. All the patients had resolved to never give up the fight.

As you come to the end of this book, you are coming to the beginning of the next chapter of your life. You are in rehabilitation. While trying to walk right, you may fall sometimes, but get back up. In trying to monitor your words, you might say the wrong thing. Your eyes will get stronger once you start looking out for self first and consider other people and the effect your decisions and actions will have upon them. Last but not least, make sure you determine in your mind not to fall for the same traps, or get into the same situations that started the conflict in the first place. Let us fight on until victory is won.

★

As you come to the end of this book, you are coming to the beginning of the next chapter of your life.

★

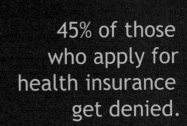

ORDER FORM

Name _____

Company _____

Address _____

City _____State_____Zip_____

Telephone _____

Email_____

Please send me_____ copies of World War Me.

Price   Shipping   Total
$15.95 $4.00 per book $19.95

Total Enclosed: $_____

Books are available at special discounts for bulk purchases, sales promotions, fundraising, or educational purposes.

For more information about the author or speaking engagements, write to:

Jamal Bryant Ministries
1505 Eutaw Place
Baltimore, MD 21217

www.jamalbryant.org
www.myspace.com/jamalbryant
www.twitter.com/jamalbryant
www.worldwarme.com